A Blandford
PET HANDBOOK

Reptiles and Amphibians

A Blandford
PET HANDBOOK

Reptiles
and Amphibians

Joan Palmer

Blandford Press
POOLE · DORSET

First published in the U.K. 1983 by Blandford Press,
Link House, West Street, Poole, Dorset, BH15 1LL

Copyright © 1983 Blandford Books Ltd

Distributed in the United States by
Sterling Publishing Co., Inc.,
2 Park Avenue, New York, N.Y. 10016

British Library Cataloguing in Publication Data

Palmer, John
    Reptiles and amphibians. — (A Blandford pet
handbook)
    1. Reptiles as pets   2. Amphibians as pets
    I. Title
    639.3'9   SF459.R4

ISBN 0 7137 1201 5

Typeset by Megaron Typesetting, Boscombe, Bournemouth

Printed by Butler & Tanner Ltd, Frome and London

Contents

Acknowledgements   6

Introduction   7

1   General care and requirements   9

2   Newts and salamanders   20

3   Frogs and toads   25

4   Alligators and crocodiles   34

5   Tortoises and terrapins   36

6   Lizards   47

7   Snakes   62

8   Recording and conserving in the wild   72

9   How to obtain your pet   79

10   Herpetological societies   81

11   Legislation   85

Useful addresses   86

References   89

Index   91

Acknowledgements

The author would like to thank the following for supplying help, information, and, above all, encouragement: Dr. Oliphant F. Jackson, MRCVS; Mr Henry Arnold (Biological Records Centre); Mrs. Pat Evans; Mr. John Crompton; The Royal Society for the Prevention of Cruelty to Animals; The People's Dispensary for Sick Animals; The Zoological Society of London.

The publishers would like to thank Christopher Mattison for supplying information and photographs.

Introduction

Some people have had a lifelong interest in reptiles and amphibians from the first time they visited a zoo, or took home a jar of spawn from the local pond. Others may have been fascinated by watching a snake, frog or toad in the wild. Others may be more fortunate in knowing a hobbyist already keeping animals of this group who can advise on a first choice of pet for the beginner.

The American Humane Association claims that reptilian pets are becoming more and more popular, while in Britain, too, the owner of a pet reptile or amphibian is becoming less of a rarity — and regarded as less of an eccentric — as more is learnt about these cleanest of animals. They can afford a great deal of pleasure if knowledgeably kept, many enjoying a lengthy lifespan, and they neither smell nor harbour fleas. If unobtrusively and intelligently managed, with due care being taken with regard to escape-proofing their quarters, they are unlikely to offend a 'no pets' rule.

In the hobby of herpetology, that is reptile-and-amphibian-keeping, it is essential, for the welfare of the animals, to be able to walk before one can run. Please do not go out and buy the first snake that you find attractive just for the sheer excitement of ownership. Many species available on the market require experience on the part of their owners if they are to survive, let alone thrive, in captivity.

Pet shops and specialist retailers are generally most helpful in advising on feeding and housing requirements for particular species, and they should tell you which are the least demanding, and most tolerant of captivity. There are societies and periodicals which prospective owners may refer to for advice, and it is most strongly recommended that a person with some experience in the hobby is available to supervise the first-time buyer.

Reptiles and amphibians are, in the main, disliked by those who are unfamiliar with them. Many are becoming endangered in the wild because of man's ignorance and prejudice against them. By gradually building up your knowledge of these animals, by displaying a respect and affection for them, you will be on your way to becoming an ambassador for a hobby which needs more friends. It is hoped that with this book you will be set on the right road to becoming a successful herpetologist.

1
General care and requirements

What are reptiles and amphibians?

This book deals with the care of two major classes of the animal
kingdom, the amphibians and the reptiles, both of which comprise
vertebrate or back-boned animals. Both classes are cold-blooded, that
is dependent on outside sources of heat to maintain their body
temperature, and it is of vital importance that the prospective owner
of one of these animals realises the implications of this fundamental
characteristic. It is essential to know the temperature and general
environmental conditions which the particular animal enjoys in its
native land, and it should be the aim of the owner to duplicate natural
conditions as far as is possible.

Amphibians

Amphibians comprise two groups commonly referred to as the newts
and salamanders, and the frogs and toads. It should be understood
that these terms are quite unscientific, but they are handy in that
common usage has ensured that most people know what is meant by
the terms without having to resort to precise classification.

In brief, newts and salamanders, belonging to the order Caudata,
are amphibians with tails. Those species living in water are known as
newts, while those which are more terrestrial are known as
salamanders.

Frogs and toads, in contrast to newts and salamanders, have no
tails: they are therefore scientifically classified in a separate order,
and this is the Anura. Again, there is a general understanding, rather

than a scientific basis for separation, that the term 'frog' refers to smooth, damp species, while the term 'toad' is reserved for dry-skinned species.

Between them, the Caudata and Anura account for about 4000 species.

Breeding from reptiles and amphibians is beyond the scope of this book, although there are works listed in the References which will give information on this aspect of the hobby for those interested in pursuing it. It is nevertheless important to understand the life-cycle of amphibians as it has a bearing on their maintenance in captivity.

The vast majority of amphibians lay eggs, or eggs in spawn, in water; after a time the eggs hatch into larvae or tadpoles, which live in water; later they undergo a transition to become small versions of the adult form, and most then live primarily on land, returning to the water to breed; some, however, remain aquatic throughout their lives, and these species obviously need to be housed in an aquarium.

Reptiles

As well as crocodiles and alligators, belonging to the order Crocodilia, which merit only a very brief mention in this book as they are quite unsuitable for private collections, the reptile class comprises the two orders Chelonia and Squamata.

Chelonians are the shelled reptiles—turtles, terrapins and tortoises—of which there are roughly 200 species; the Squamata comprises two very separate groups—the lizards and the snakes—together totalling some 5700 species. In most cases it is obvious from the lack of limbs that a species is a snake and not a lizard, but there are some limbless lizards, classified as such rather than as snakes because of their external ears and their movable eyelids.

Among the snakes are the most famous and sensational of all reptiles, the venomous species, which have been responsible for much of the prejudice against all reptiles which still prevails all over the world. Venomous snakes puncture the skin with hollow fangs through which poison from sacs located in the snake's head is injected into the victim's bloodstream killing body tissue and paralysing. The main families of the venomous group are cobras, coral snakes and mambas which belong to the Elapidae, vipers which belong to the Viperidae, and its sub-family, the Crotalinae, which takes in rattle-snakes, cottonmouths and tropical pit vipers. *On no account should these species be kept by amateurs.* It is necessary in any case, in the UK and the USA, to hold a licence to keep dangerous animals, and the requirements to be fulfilled are unlikely to be met by beginners.

Before deciding on which type of reptile or amphibian to keep you should compare the various requirements given in the chapters on particular groups. You will have several major considerations and these are outlined below.

Accommodation

Will the animal require a vivarium or an aquarium? What temperature of air and water will it require? Do you have only indoor facilities or can you consider using a greenhouse, or hutch in the garden. How are you going to heat the accommodation? Will you need to spray heated vivariums to maintain a high humidity?

General information on how to supply the basic requirements is given below but models of vivarium will need to be adapted with reference to the chapters giving details for individual species (see also Figures 1 and 2.

Figure 1 A standard moist vivarium showing vegetation suitable for toads and salamanders hailing from woodland habitats

Figure 2 Suitable basking sites can easily be provided for species used to desert or arid conditions. Many lizards and small snakes will do well in vivariums such as this

The framework for your accommodation will probably be some sort of rectangular 'box', whether it is long and low or tall and narrow, with an escape-proof lid. It may be made of glass, perspex, metal, plastic or wood, and there are various advantages and disadvantages in using any of these materials. The important considerations are that the material used should be capable of being heated, furnished, ventilated and humidified appropriately.

By reference to the lists of species suited to captivity you will see what are the preferred temperature ranges of individuals. These temperatures may be provided by various means including soil-warming cables of the type used in greenhouses, and infra-red lamps or light bulbs suspended above the vivarium. A thermostat will be necessary to control the temperature. You will need to seek the advice of manufacturers of this specialist equipment to make sure that your chosen heat source is compatible with the material of which the accommodation is made, the lighting which the animal finds comfortable, and the degree of humidity which it requires. Remember that for those creatures which bask, a hot spot and a relatively cooler area will be needed within the confines of the accommodation.

Ready-made aquariums are more likely to be available than cages for terrestrial species, and a visit to your local tropical fish retailer should give you ideas on how the accommodation readily available can be adapted for amphibians. Many species will require both dry land and access to water (see Figure 3) and may need areas where they can be submerged but breathe air, so that varying depths of water should be available. Make sure that the accommodation you acquire can be adapted to provide for these necessities.

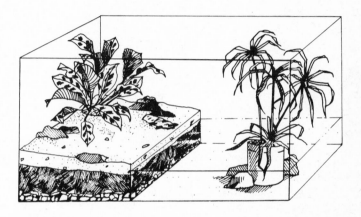

Figure 3 If part of the ground area of a glass vivarium is filled with gravel and soil and part left for water, an attractive semi-aquatic habitat can be duplicated quite simply

Having purchased or made the basic cage, and filled it to an appropriate depth with water or sand, gravel, paper, or whatever is recommended for your pet, you will need to furnish it further with plants, rocks and twigs which will create as near natural an environment as possible. If the notes for individual species mention that they are shy, do not forget to provide areas of dense vegetation or small 'caves' in which they can hide. If they are arboreal they will need tall vivariums which should have twigs up which they can climb (see Figure 4).

Figure 4 Variations on the theme shown here can be achieved by creative use of plants and twigs or branches. Tall vivariums can be densely or thinly planted depending on the shyness of the species being housed

Feeding

Is the pet a herbivore or a carnivore, or will it require a mixed diet? Is the suitable food easily available from pet shops or will you have to breed your own, and if so will you have room for the breeding cages or tanks as well as the vivarium for the pet? If your pet requires fresh mice or rats will you be prepared to kill them? Perhaps you will be able to collect food for your pet, but do you have the time always to do this when it is necessary?

You will need to refer to the details on individual species to discover the particular preferences of your chosen pet but below are given guidelines to help you assess what is likely to be required of you in feeding your specimen.

First and foremost, please ensure that your pet always has water available, and that it can reach the source. It will probably be best to sink a dish in the sand or other substrate on the floor of the vivarium. As some species prefer to lap moisture from foliage it is a good idea to spray the vivarium so that the leaves always remain wet.

The large snakes have an enormous swallowing and digesting capacity and need to be fed only quite infrequently—depending on the species it might be once, twice or three times a week, and some will need to be fed even less frequently than that. Most reptiles and amphibians, however, will need feeding every day: at first it is best to err on the side of generous feeding and when it is noticed that food is left over the timings and quantities can be adjusted accordingly. It is obviously important to keep exact records of what and when food is being provided.

It is useless to purchase any animal if you cannot, or will not, provide the right food for it. As an example you should not obtain any species of vine snake—which can only survive on tree lizards—if this food is unavailable. Similarly if you are squeamish about breeding rodents for consumption, you should not acquire a rodent-eating snake. If, however, you do acquire one, you will have to learn to keep and breed mice for the snake's consumption, bearing in mind that, as the snake grows bigger, the mice must be replaced by rats and that larger boxes will be required for them accordingly.

Contrary to common belief, rats and mice should *never be fed alive*—indeed in most places this is illegal—but despatched quickly and humanely beforehand. Dead feeding is advocated for two reasons—not merely dislike of the idea that it is a showpiece for the snake to kill in one stroke, but because diseases can be transmitted to snakes by intestinal bacteria. If, for instance, you were to put a live mouse, or rat, into the snake's enclosure, it would urinate and defaecate over the area, so that, before long, the snake would contract skin disease from crawling over the strata on which the faeces and urine has been passed.

Quick, sharp killing of the rodent is advocated and if it is slipped into the vivarium while fresh the snake will throw a coil round the offering as if it had made a kill, and the feeding process will take place quite normally. But do remember that if the snake is not hungry it will not eat, so you must then think in terms of taking the dead body out.

If you propose to breed mice, ideally you should start with two female mice and one male, providing another box in which to house the weaned babies. In this way, mindful that mice can breed every 21 days, you will rapidly produce sufficient food for one snake.

The wooden mouse boxes, which can have either a glass or wire front should be lined with sawdust, hay or straw being provided for bedding. It is essential that the mouse boxes are cleaned out regularly, that fresh water is always provided for the inhabitants and that they are fed daily with almost any household scraps except meat or fat.

Other animal food may be bred for consumption, or may be purchased as required. It suits most people best to purchase food, mealworms, locusts, crickets, whiteworms and maggots being available from dealers in tropical fish or from reptile dealers (see Figures 5, 6 and 7). As a standby supply you may wish to breed some creatures and mealworms, the larvae of the Flour Beetle, can easily be bred from a few of the adult beetles placed in a tub of meal with a dish of water. The eggs which the adults will lay will take about three months to grow into sizeable mealworms. A few left to develop into adults will ensure the continuation of the culture.

Figure 5 The Locust, Schistocerca gregaria

Figure 6 Crickets, Gryllus bimaculatus

Figure 7 Mealworms, the larvae of Tenebrio molitor, *the Flour Beetle*

Although it is unlikely that you will regularly be able to collect live food, the occasional offering of a varied dish of invertebrates will be appreciated. You can collect them from a pond or stream or by sweeping through long grass with a net.

Reptiles and amphibians which are herbivorous as opposed to carnivorous are rather easier to cater for, but remember to supply a varied diet of green food and soft fruit, and it is perhaps even more important for these animals than for the meat-eaters to provide multi-vitamin supplements in the form of Vionate or Abidec. Even though your pet may appear in the best of health it is as well to obviate vitamin and mineral deficiency problems by regularly feeding supplements.

It is a good idea, apart from adding yet another interesting aspect to the hobby of reptile-keeping to check the growth, weight, and eating habits of pets, as it enables the owner to note from his records when anything is amiss. Having determined the correct weight for an individual the owner is enabled to take action where, for example, a dramatic loss occurs, and to vary diet accordingly and/or seek veterinary aid.

A good idea is to keep a ledger or exercise book, and to retain therein a record of each pet and its progress from the time of purchase or hatching. Such an entry would be headed perhaps with the name and type of pet, the date, and where purchased/hatched, and its body weight at the time of initial weighing.

Columns can then be added so that the owner may enter at fort-nightly intervals, or such periods as he may decide, the date and food given; for instance, one rabbit, half a dozen whitebait or whatever the meal may have comprised, and the weight and measurement at that date. Information on longevity in captivity should also be useful enabling the hobbyist to look back over a period of years noting the feeding and other practices which have met with success and, no doubt, learning as most of us do from earlier mistakes.

It is helpful also to record, in addition to the weights and measure-ments, the diseases which have been encountered, together with notes on the treatments advocated and the creature's responses. A record such as this may prove invaluable.

It is obvious that the more information of this type that is avail-able, the easier the task of the veterinary surgeon will be in pin-pointing and correcting any ailment or deficiency which may arise in the future.

Finance

Please consider carefully the long-term as well as the short-term requirements of your pet. As well as the initial outlay on purchasing the animal and its vivarium along with the plants, lights, and heating equipment, you will have to always be able to afford its basic food, its heating bills and its vitamin supplements. However solicitous you are in its management, there may be times when you need to seek professional veterinary advice, and this will involve a consultation fee as well as the purchase price of medication. If you are away from home at any time you may have to make arrangements for someone to look after your pet, and this may cost something.

It is highly irresponsible to acquire a pet of any sort before looking into all the implications of keeping it in a suitable environment with suitable food. Similarly you should never consider giving any sort of pet as a gift. It is only the person who has to look after the animal who can judge whether he has the ability and the desire to look after it properly.

Now that you are aware of the general areas of care, you can consider the details for the various groups discussed in the following chapters: there are many to choose from so make sure that you can give adequate attention to whichever pet you decide upon.

2
Newts and salamanders

As explained in Chapter 1, it is popular usage which has given us the categories we call newts and salamanders, both groups being tailed amphibians—the newts commonly being thought of as aquatic, and the salamanders, while recognised as liking damp conditions, being the more terrestrial relatives. Salamanders are found in rivers, streams, swamps and ditches as well as in ponds and moist woodlands. Although often mistaken for lizards, salamanders have a smooth, moist, non-scaly, skin. Most have four toes on their front feet and five on their hind feet, make no sound and neither do they have ears.

Figure 8 Fire Salamander, Salamandra salamandra. *This is the subspecies* S.s. terrestris *found in France*

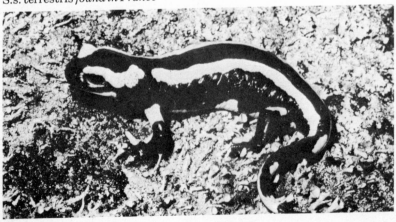

Both newts and salamanders are popular as pets and are, on the whole, fairly undemanding creatures.

There are three main families from this order whose representatives are found in captivity. The mole salamanders, of which the Axolotl is perhaps the best known example, and the woodland salamanders are almost exclusively North American, while the true salamanders are more cosmopolitan, hailing from Europe and Asia as well as North America.

Accommodation

Salamanders and newts can be kept together with other amphibians if you wish, and do best in a large aquarium, preferably with a cover of perforated zinc, or similar material to prevent escape.

Land-type salamanders and red efts need dark, moist homes with places to hide under plants, mosses, rocks, bark or logs.

A glass or plastic aquarium or an old sink will be ideal. Half fill this with pond water, from the original habitat if possible, and include plenty of water-weed to provide shelter. Floating rafts of thin cork will allow the amphibians to leave the water if they wish.

Aquaria should be kept cool and certainly out of direct sunlight and it is a good idea to embed the sink, or glass aquarium, in the ground in a sheltered outdoor position, keeping it well protected by a secure perforated zinc or metal mesh cover.

Figure 9 *Japanese Fire-bellied Newt,* Cynops pyrrhogaster

The water in the aquarium must be changed once a week, and it is essential to wash your hands after undertaking this task, or handling your pets, mindful that there is a risk of contracting salmonella from dirty water and that some creatures, for instance fire salamanders, emit a poisonous secretion from the skin.

Feeding

Salamandridae are, in the main, nocturnal and in the evening hours will delight in seeking out the titbits which you have provided.

Worms, small insects, small spiders and chopped lean beef or liver once a week would prove an excellent diet. But slugs, caterpillars and woodlice will also be welcomed as will greenfly. The large salamander will eat a small mouse and newts and salamanders will consume with relish such foods as brineshrimp, white worm, tubifex and small earthworms which should be readily available from your pet store.

Figure 10 Axolotl, Ambystoma mexicanum. *This shows the white phase; black phase specimens are also available*

Figure 11 Palmate Newt, Triturus helveticus. *This specimen is a breeding male*

List of Newts and Salamanders Suited to Captivity

Terrestrial Species

Red Eft 8 cm (3 in)
Diemictylus viridescens

Damp vivarium, 15° — 20°C (59° — 68°F); feed earthworms, maggots. This is the larval form of the aquatic Red-spotted Newt.

Spotted Salamander 15 cm (6 in)
Ambystoma maculatum

Damp vivarium, shady, 15° — 20°C (59° — 68°F), with moss and ferns; feed earthworms, slugs, insects.

Tiger Salamander 15 cm (6 in)
Ambystoma tigrinum

Damp vivarium, shady, 20° — 25°C (68° — 77°F), with moss and ferns; feed earthworms and large insects.

Fire Salamander 20 cm (8 in)
Salamandra salamandra
(See Figure 8)

Damp vivarium, cool and very shady, 15°C (59°F), with moss and ferns; feed earthworms, slugs, larvae. This species is nocturnal by nature so will appreciate shade and hiding places.

Aquatic Species

Red-spotted Newt 8 cm (3 in)
Diemictylus viridescens

Cool aquarium with pebbles and plants; feed earthworms, tubifex worms, maggots.

Japanese Fire-bellied Newt 10 cm (4 in)
Cynops pyrrhogaster
(See Figure 9)

Cool aquarium, planted if possible; feed earthworms, tubifex worms, maggots.

Axolotl 20 cm (8 in)
Ambystoma mexicanum
(See Figure 10)

Aquarium, 15° − 20°C (59° − 68°F); feed earthworms, mealworms, small pieces meat. Black and white colour variations of this species exist.

Ribbed Salamander 25 cm (10 in)
Pleurodeles walt

Cool aquarium, add pebbles and plants for decoration; feed earthworms, maggots, tubifex worms.

Semi-aquatic Species

Palmate Newt 8 cm (3 in)
Triturus helveticus
(See Figure 11)

Aquarium, 20°C (68°F), planted and with island; feed earthworms, tubifex worms, insects.

Marbled Newt 10 cm (4 in)
Triturus marmoratus

Very moist vivarium, shady, 20°C (68°F) with moss and ferns; feed earthworms, maggots, insects.

Smooth Newt 8 cm (3 in)
Triturus vulgaris

Aquarium, 20°C (68°F), planted and with mossy rocks jutting out as island; feed earthworms, tubifex worms, insects.

Alpine Newt 10 cm (4 in)
Triturus alpestris

Aquarium, 20°C (68°F), planted and with mossy rocks jutting out of water for island; feed earthworms, tubifex worms, insects.

Crested Newt 12 cm (5 in)
Triturus cristatus

Aquarium, 20°C (68°F) with mossy island; feed earthworms, tubifex worms, insects.

3
Frogs and toads

Frogs and toads are similar in that they are both groups of tailless amphibians. Frogs tend to be slimmer and longer-limbed than toads, and their skin is moister and smoother. Toads' skin feels drier and rougher because of the presence of warts. Their tongues are rounded at the end and the males have a swollen nuptial pad on each first finger which darkens during the breeding season. On the whole, toads do well in captivity, being intelligent and making good pets, some coming to hand for their food.

As with newts and salamanders, the frogs and toads, or Anura as they are scientifically classified, have some members which are entirely aquatic, and though most will thrive in a terrarium, all should have access to some damp or wet area.

There are several families of frog and toad coming from all over the world's temperate and tropical zones and they vary enormously in attractiveness of appearance as well as in their requirements in captivity. Tree-frogs are perhaps the most discrete group among this order, and many are quite amenable to captivity so long as opportunity is given for them to climb. They have been a very successful group in the wild, and are found in Australasia, Europe, Africa and the Americas. The ranids, among which are found the true frogs, and the bufonids, or true toads, are also large and extremely successful families, being found all over the world. Another group to be found among the ranids are the poison arrow frogs which are very colourful and otherwise attractive specimens whose skin contains a potentially dangerous poison. Other major families are not well represented by species available for captivity though a few will be mentioned in the list of species on page 30.

Accommodation

Frogs and toads need a 'large' home. Don't mix species unless you know their habits and don't put large ones and small ones together or they might eat each other. You must also check carefully as to the requirements of species imported from the tropics as some of these such as the Giant Toad and certain tree frogs need peat.

A good rule of thumb is to provide a habitat for terrestrial creatures that is mostly land area with a small fresh pool, and a habitat for aquatic creatures that has a large water area with a small dry land island. A covered, well ventilated aquarium or terrarium is best. Bear in mind, however, that frogs are not as intelligent as toads and never seem to learn that glass is a barrier through which they cannot jump.

To make a pond and island habitat, fill a deep plastic or glass container, which will serve as your pet's island, with a layer of charcoal, 2—3 cm (1 in) of coarse sand, pebbles or aquarium gravel and finally a mixture of peat, moss and loam. Add small plants, bark, small logs, rocks and moss. Place this island at one end of the aquarium and lean a rock against it so your pet can climb out of the water easily. Fill with water to just below the island level. Let tap water sit for two days then place in the aquarium, or use pond water.

Figure 12 Pacific Tree Frog, regilla *Figure 13 Grey Tree Frog*, Hyla versicolor

The land and pond habitat is the reverse recipe of the pond and island habitat and uses the same material from one end of the aquarium to the other. One end should be about 2–5 cm (1–2 in) higher than the other end. Again, furnish with plants, rocks, moss, bark and small logs. At the bottom of the slope place a small glass or plastic container, which will serve as the pet's pond area. Put a layer of coarse sand or gravel in the bottom and fill with pond water. Add rocks around the pool so that your pet can climb out easily and be sure to keep the water clean.

Whichever habitat you attempt to reproduce perhaps the most important thing is not to let the accommodation dry out.

Feeding

Frogs and toads are relatively easy creatures to keep well fed, and though you should pay attention to any particular points mentioned in the list of species on page 30, the general guidelines are simple. Insects, earthworms, spiders, snails and mealworms will be taken, and pieces of meat and fish will also be appreciated: it is a good idea to simulate movement in the food when offering it as this may encourage slow feeders.

Figure 14 Marbled Reed Frog, Hyperolius marmoratus *Figure 15 Gulf Coast Toad,* Bufo valliceps, *an African species of this cosmopolitan genus, requiring conditions similar to those for* B. americanus

Figure 16 Clawed Toad, Xenopus laevis

Figure 17 Oriental Fire-bellied Toad, Bombina orientalis

Figure 18 Giant Fire-bellied Toad, Bombina maxima, *a semi-aquatic species sometimes available for captivity*

Ailments

Fungal skin diseases are perhaps the most common ailment of this group, and these can be caused by overcrowding, foul water, incorrect feeding or bad ventilation. You should check each of these possible causes and remedy them immediately if any of them is at fault. Contact your veterinary surgeon, too, to investigate medication for the problem.

Abrasions may be treated by antibiotic powder or an iodine solution such as Betadine, and a disease known as redleg (reddening of the inside of the hindleg), peculiar to frogs, will often respond to antibiotics.

Anurans will thrive in damp conditions; never expose any pet of this group to a direct heat source, including direct sunlight, or it will quickly start to fail.

Figure 19 European Common Frog, Rana temporaria

List of Frogs and Toads Suited to Captivity

Terrestrial Species

Barking Frog 2 cm (1 in)
*Eleutherodactylus
augusti*

Vivarium, 23°C (73°F), shady and with hiding places; feed small insects.

Ornate Chorus Frog 2 cm (1 in)
Pseudacris ornata

Moist vivarium, 27°C (80°F), densely planted and with mossy ground; feed small insects.

Strecker's Chorus Frog 2 cm (1 in) *Pseudacris streckeri*	Moist vivarium, 27°C (80°F), densely planted, a small pond can be provided; feed small insects.
Squirrel Tree Frog 2 cm (1 in) *Hyla squirella*	Tall vivarium, 27°C (80°F), with branches for climbing; feed small insects and flies.
Lovely Poison Arrow Frog 2.5 cm (1 in) *Phyllobates lugubris*	Tall vivarium, 27°C (80°F), with dense vegetation and humid; feed small insects.
Yellow-banded Poison Arrow Frog 3 cm (1 in) *Dendrobates leucomelas*	Tall vivarium, 27°C (80°F), with vegetation, humid; feed insects.
Green Poison Arrow Frog 3 cm (1 in) *Dendrobates auratus*	Tall vivarium, 27°C (80°F) with dense vegetation, humid; feed insects.
Pacific Tree Frog 3 cm (1 in) *Hyla regilla* (See Figure 12)	Tall vivarium or greenhouse, 23°C (73°F) with branches for climbing and dense vegetation; feed flies and other insects.
Red-eyed Tree Frog 3 cm (1 in) *Agalychnis callidryas*	Tall vivarium, 23°C (73°F), humid, planted well, add branches for climbing; feed flies and other insects.
Spring Peeper 3 cm (1 in) *Hyla crucifer*	Tall vivarium, 23°C (73°F), densely planted and with bark and boughs; feed flies and other insects.
European Tree Frog 4 cm (2 in) *Hyla arborea*	Tall vivarium, 23°C (73°F), or greenhouse, with branches, and well planted; feed flies and other insects.
Grey Tree Frog 4 cm (2 in) *Hyla versicolor* (See Figure 13)	Tall vivarium, 23°C (73°F), or greenhouse, with branches; feed flies and other insects.
Reed Frogs 4 cm (2 in) *Hyperolius* spp. (See Figure 14)	Tall, humid, vivarium, 25°C (77°F), with small pond, and densely planted; feed flies and other insects.

African Grey Tree Frog 5 cm (2 in) *Chiromantis xerampelina*	Tall vivarium, 23°C (73°F), with branches for climbing and densely planted; feed flies and other insects.
Asian Bullfrog 7 cm (3 in) *Kaloula pulchra*	Moist vivarium with stones and logs, 26°C (78°F), with mossy ground; feed large insects.
White's Tree Frog 8 cm (3 in) *Litoria caerulea*	Tall vivarium, 27°C (80°F), well planted and with branches for climbing; feed small pieces meat and large insects.
Asiatic Horned Toad 8 cm (3 in) *Megophrys nasuta*	Moist vivarium with hiding places, 24°C (75°F), with leafy ground; feed large insects.
American Toad 8 cm (3 in) *Bufo americanus* (See Figure 15)	Warm vivarium, 20°C (68°F), or greenhouse, with mossy ground and hiding places; feed small pieces meat, large insects, larvae and earthworms.
Green Toad 8 cm (3 in) *Bufo viridis*	Moist vivarium, cool, with cover and sandy ground; feed insects and larvae.
Western Toad 10 cm (4 in) *Bufo boreas*	Vivarium, cool, with mossy ground and some cover; feed insects and larvae and small pieces of meat.
European Common Toad 12 cm (5 in) *Bufo bufo*	Vivarium, cool, with stones and logs for cover; feed insects, maggots, small pieces of meat.

Aquatic Species

Dwarf Clawed Toad 3 cm (1 in) *Hymenochirus boettgeri*	Aquarium, 23°C (74°F), shady; feed worms, maggots, pieces of meat or fish.
Clawed Toad 12 cm (5 in) *Xenopus laevis* (See Figure 16)	Aquarium, 23°C (74°F), with pebbles; feed worms, pieces of meat or fish.
Surinam Toad 15 cm (6 in) *Pipa pipa*	Aquarium, 28°C (83°F), well planted; feed fish and pieces of meat.

Semi-aquatic Species

Fire-bellied Toad 4 cm (2 in)
Bombina bombina

Aquarium, cool, with islands and floating plants. Provide refuges for this shy species; feed insects and small pieces of meat.

Yellow-bellied Toad 4 cm (2 in)
Bombina variegata

Aquarium, cool, with islands and hiding places, or treat as terrestrial (vivarium with bark and moss); feed on insects and small pieces of meat.

Oriental Fire-bellied Toad 6 cm (2½ in)
Bombina orientalis
(See Figures 17 and 18)

Aquarium, cool, with hiding places or treat as terrestrial (vivarium with bark and moss); feed insects and small pieces of meat.

Painted Frog 6 cm (2½ in)
Discoglossus pictus

Aquarium, cool, with plenty of shelter and rocky and mossy islands; feed small fish and insects.

European Common Frog 8 cm (3 in)
Rana temporaria
(See Figure 19)

Aquarium, cool, with plenty of shelter and rocky and mossy islands; feed small fish and insects.

Leopard Frog 8 cm (3 in)
Rana pipiens

Aquarium, cool, with some islands; feed insects.

Marsh Frog 10 cm (4 in)
Rana ridibunda

Aquarium, cool, planted and with pebbles; feed insects and earthworms.

Bullfrog 20 cm (8 in)
Rana catesbiana

Large vivarium, cool, planted and with loose soil, pond also, with floating plants; feed fish, pieces of meat, insects, and earthworms.

African Bullfrog 20 cm (8 in)
Pyxicephalus adspersus

Vivarium, cool, with loose mossy ground; also pond; feed pieces of meat, insects, and earthworms.

4

Alligators and crocodiles

It is not recommended that beginning herpetologists or indeed private collectors of any degree of experience should keep crocodiles or alligators. All species are protected throughout the world, and in Britain the possession of one requires a licence under the Dangerous Wild Animals Act 1976. The information given here is for interest only and may serve to explain why these animals are unsuitable pets.

Alligators

The alligator, in common with the crocodile, can easily outgrow its allotted living quarters and great care must be taken in handling, for although some subjects do indeed become quite tame there are others which are prodigious biters.

The American alligator inhabits swamps and creeks, growing to a final length of 5 m (15 ft) or even more, its growth rate being approximately 30 cm (1 ft) per year, slowing down as it reaches maturity.

Accommodation for this animal should ideally be a large aquarium with the water and air temperature maintained at around 27° (80°F). Below this temperature there may be a reluctance to eat. The water should be only 15 cm (6 in) or so in depth with pebbles arranged at one end, so as to offer a resting place out of the water. In the wild the alligator's diet consists of birds, fish and small mammals, but it will feed, in captivity, on worms, insects and frogs. It can also be tempted by tropical fish.

The alligator is an intelligent animal which, in ideal conditions, can live for many years. It should, however, not be bought as a pet; even some zoos cannot provide adequate space to allow for its rapid growth.

Crocodiles

The crocodile is perhaps more feared than the alligator: it is a large, amphibious thick-skinned and long-tailed reptile, and although some are tameable, many are never to be trusted.

Crocodiles grow rapidly and are entirely unsuitable for captivity in a domestic environment. They need an air and water temperature of 27−32°C (80−90°F), plenty of direct sunlight and must be kept alone. They fight with their fellows. Because crocodiles grow so rapidly they have a strong requirement for calcium as part of their diet. When they are in the wild they will seize a whole fish. If they happen to find some animal on the river bank they will take the whole animal as well and are able to digest the skeleton. However, in captivity one tends to feed crocodiles meat which is calcium and Vitamin A deficient. This problem along with that of accommodation makes the crocodile a most unsuitable pet.

5

Tortoises and terrapins

The order Chelonia comprises the shelled reptiles, turtles, tortoises and terrapins: they can boast ancestors which roamed the earth as long ago as two million years. Their lifespan can be as long as 100 years in captivity and stories abound as to the longevity of individual specimens. Alas, however, nobody has been around long enough to vouch for their authenticity!

It is as well to clarify what we mean by giving the three groups of chelonians separate common names. Tortoises are land animals, known in parts of America as land turtles; terrapins are freshwater creatures, and turtles are marine. These last are quite unsuitable for private collections owing to the large size which they attain. In fact it is a matter of some debate whether chelonians should be available in the pet trade at all as so many of them die during shipment from their native lands.

Tortoises and terrapins look similar, and both originate from warm climates. As reptiles they are unable to control their body temperature, depending entirely on the warmth of their surroundings for the ability to move, eat and grow, and the proverbial slow, pet tortoise can in fact move quite quickly in its native climate. It belongs to hot, dry lands such as North Africa and Greece and is mainly vegetarian. Many of the terrapins on the other hand come from hot, wet tropical marshes, ponds and river-banks where they live in and out of the water, swimming and feeding on snails, frogs, worms and fish. The tortoise cannot live the life of a terrapin nor a terrapin the life of a tortoise, so it is essential to be able to distinguish the terrapin with its rather flat shell and its 'webbed feet' from the land tortoise with its domed and deeply patterned shell.

It is not easy to breed these reptiles in cold temperate regions, but one wishes that the practice were more common in that those imported from other lands frequently arrive in an unsatisfactory condition often having been packed one on top of the other in boxes.

Tortoises

In Britain the tortoise has now been listed as an endangered species and buyers must sign an official declaration when making their purchase to the effect that they will look after it correctly according to the information sheet supplied and understand that the conditions under which the tortoise is kept should be open to inspection at any time.

Please do not contemplate buying a tortoise later than June, earlier if you can. Delay may result in your tortoise having insufficient time in which to acclimatise itself, or to eat sufficient to enable it to survive the long winter hibernation. When you buy, make sure that your choice is alert and bright eyed, and that the nose and nostrils are clean and the shell free from cracks. Also, examine the legs and neck to make sure that they are free from ticks.

Figure 20 Hermann's Tortoise, Testudo hermanni

Types and sexing

There are several types of tortoise throughout the world. However, those which most frequently find their way into pet outlets are the Mediterranean Spur-Thighed Tortoise (*Testudo graeca*), whose natural habitat is the shores of the Mediterranean Sea; and which is imported from Tunisia and Morocco—although also from Spain, Greece, Turkey and Romania—and the Hermann's Tortoise (*Testudo hermanni*) (see Figure 20) which also inhabits the shores of the Mediterranean, but mostly on the Italian and Yugoslav coasts.

The Mediterranean Spur-Thighed Tortoise carries a spur on the inner aspect of the thighs and this is its main distinguishing feature. Hermann's Tortoise has a claw-like appendage on the tip of the tail. There is little difference in the appearance of the shell of the two types.

There is no reliable method of telling a tortoise's age, the so-called rings, unlike the proverbial tree-trunk, being no accurate guide whatsoever. However, do not choose one which measures less than 10 cm (4 in) across the shell underneath, since a well-grown imported tortoise stands a far better chance of survival than a very young one.

Sex, on the other hand, is easily determined (see Figure 21). The undershell or plastron in the female is flat, or may be slightly convex, whilst in the male it may be slightly concave. The tail of the female is short, whereas in the male it is rather long and curved but you do need to see both male and female tortoises to compare. Many a supposedly male tortoise has produced eggs within a few weeks of importation and sale!

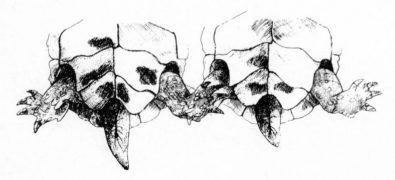

Figure 21 The male tortoise, on the left, has a longer and more curved tail than the female, shown right

Hibernation

Do remember that individual tortioses will hibernate at different times and that each one will vary as to its time of awakening. The weather varies so much throughout temperate regions that a definite indication cannot be given. By about October, however, most tortoises will become sluggish and indifferent to food. This is a sure sign that they should be allowed to go without food for three weeks or so, to clear their digestive system before commencing their long, winter sleep.

The house the tortoise has inhabited during the summer may be used for hibernation, but a specially prepared box is more suitable. (It should be in the region of 30 000 cc [1 cu. ft] capacity for each tortoise). Place about 5 cm (2 in) of dry leaves, or hay, in the bottom. Place the tortoise in this and then completely surround the pet to a depth of about 8 cm (3 in) with the same bedding. Now cover the top of the box with fine wire mesh, or a perforated wooden lid so that the box is ventilated but rat-proof and place it in a cold shed, or outhouse, which is frost proof.

This done, the tortoise may be left to sleep peacefully until about March.

With the approach of spring the tortoise will gradually return to activity and your attention will be needed. For instance, if the mouth and eyes have become glued up, bathe them gently with warm water to wash away congealed mucus; if necessary treat the nostrils similarly.

Fresh drinking water will be appreciated at this time and your tortoise will not be averse to a warm bath to help with the waking process. To bath, place the tortoise in a large dish containing about 4 cm (1½ in) of lukewarm water (about 29°C [85°F]), so that the lower part of the body is immersed, but the head can be kept clear. About 5–10 minutes should be sufficient.

At first leave the tortoise outside only during the sunnier part of the day. Only when the weather has become reasonably warm and the tortoise is active can it be allowed to stay out permanently.

Information sheets currently being provided in the United Kingdom suggest that provided tortoises are kept in centrally heated accommodation it is possible to keep them awake throughout the winter and this procedure has in a number of cases proved to be satisfactory. However, it must be remembered that hibernation is a normal part of the tortoise's life cycle and it is generally believed that those tortoises kept unnaturally awake may become more sluggish than their fellows who have hibernated, and will at any rate have a reduced lifespan.

Accommodation

Tortoises are voracious eaters of plants and garden produce, so care must be taken to keep them from flower beds and kitchen gardens. If they are allowed to roam on the lawn, this should be wired off with netting of 23 — 30 cm (9 — 12 in) height, remembering that tortoises are great climbers and that their weight will soon bend wire down if it is not well supported.

In the absence of fencing, a large wooden pen can be provided which again should be surrounded by wire mesh. However, this type of construction must be portable so that it can be moved to different parts of the garden. Indeed, the type of run used for domestic rabbits often proves most suitable.

Because of tortoises' love of climbing, a rockery, albeit transportable, within the enclosure, would be greatly appreciated.

A shelter must be provided, offering your pet protection from rain, wind and sun. A wooden box resembling a small dog kennel would be ideal, raised a little off the ground with a small ramp up to the entrance. Provide lots of hay and dry leaves for bedding and hang a piece of sacking over the entrance at night to add warmth.

Feeding

Tortoises are generally thought of as vegetarian, but the Hermann's Tortoise, in particular, enjoys tackling scraps of bones and meat put out for the birds; even fish in the diet is appreciated and sometimes a little canned dog or cat food.

Obviously, fresh water must at all times be available and is best kept in a shallow dish sunk level with the surrounding ground in a shaded part of the garden. If it is not sunk the tortoise is liable to knock it over, and he will in any case probably bath in it.

Your tortoise will not eat slugs or insects but will enjoy lettuce, cabbage, sprouts, spinach, watercress, dandelions, tomatoes, peas, peapods, clover, apples and strawberries, in fact almost anything that can be found in the garden. Don't feed rhubarb leaves. They relish brown bread and jam and no doubt owners will find other delicacies that their individual pets like, but all too often when it is found that a creature has a penchant for a particular food, the owner feeds it on little else to the detriment of the pet's health. Remember to supply a varied diet at all times.

Breeding
It is not uncommon for the female tortoise soon after purchase to produce a clutch of about six or seven eggs. Usually she will deposit these in a hole, which she has dug in soft ground, afterwards covering them up, so that often they go undetected. However, you may see her deposit them, at perhaps 15 minute intervals, in her enclosure.

Now in her native land the heat of the sun could incubate the eggs but in a colder climate this does not happen naturally; and although the eggs may not all be fertile an effort should be made to hatch them out. If possible the eggs should be left in the position in which they were laid — a reptile's egg should never be turned — but transferred to a box of dry soil, or sand, which should surround them to a thickness of about 5 cm (2 in). A shoe box would, for instance, be ideal in size to contain six or seven eggs. If they are then kept at a steady temperature of $27° - 29°C$ ($80° - 85°F$) without disturbance, they should incubate in about eleven weeks. If the temperature is slightly below this suggested level the eggs may still hatch, but the incubation period will be longer.

All being well, the effort of the baby tortoise trying to free itself from the shell will raise it to the surface of the sand, hatching taking place within a couple of hours.

Housing, feeding and care of baby tortoises: For the next twelve months the baby tortoises must be kept at a temperature of approximately $21° - 24°C$ ($70° - 75°F$). Indeed, it is recommended that a heated house be built for them offering adequate space for these very active babies who love to clamber over rocks and stones just as their parents do.

There is in Surrey, England, a Mrs Pat Evans, who has met with considerable success in tortoise breeding and, by pursuing a child-hood hobby, emerged as something of an authority on tortoise pets. Her advice is that once baby tortoises have hatched, they should be fed on exactly the same food as adult tortoises. However, the rations should be chopped into tiny portions because the babies are only about 3 cm (1 in) across when they emerge, and although they do like to tear at larger pieces of green stuff, it is advisable to chop it initially and also to lace the chopped food with vitamin powders well disguised.

Additives such as Vionate and Stress (a product widely recommended for rearing puppies) are recommended, as are multivitamins, all of which should be available from pet stores. Calcium lactate tablets crushed up and mixed in with the food are essential, while some owners give their young tortoises drops of cod liver oil. However, they are very fussy and, if they smell anything like a fishy oil, are bound to avoid it studiously. At all costs, however, the young tortoises must be kept feeding or they will quickly slip into decline.

Ailments
Cracks or other shell injuries which expose tissue should be dressed with flavine oil emulsion.

Ticks covering legs and neck should be treated with an insect powder containing gammexane allowing the ticks to be removed with tweezers an hour later.

If the tortoise's eyes and mouth are sealed with mucus these should be bathed with warm water, and a mild antiseptic applied. Yellow oxide of mercury (Golden Eye Ointment) is effective. However, this is in many places now available only on prescription, so a visit to the veterinary surgeon will be necessary.

Sadly, tortoises can suffer from gangrene, an unpleasant sloughing of the skin round the head, and this is usually incurable.

Never try to put a tortoise to sleep yourself or allow one to be placed in a chlorcform lethal chamber. A barbiturate must be injected underneath the skin by a qualified veterinary surgeon, and indeed if there is doubt as to your pet's health it is best to consult a veterinarian, and soon.

Terrapins

Types and sexing
Terrapins can be distinguished from the land tortoise by their flatter shell, webbed feet and longer tail.

The terrapins most readily available are the European Pond Tortoise, *Emys orbicularis*, which is black in colour with small yellow spots or radiating lines; the Spanish Terrapin, *Mauremys caspica*, which is brownish yellow with a striped neck, and the Elegant Terrapins (*Chrysemys* species) which are greenish and have green heads, some with red markings near the eyes. The newly hatched young of this last variety are sometimes erroneously sold as miniatures. In fact, these terrapins can grow to 15 — 18 cm (6 — 7 in) in length.

It is extremely difficult to sex young terrapins, but in older pets this can, as with tortoises, be determined by the length and the shape of the tail. The tail of the male is fairly long, thick and pointed, with the vent some distance from the shell, while that of the female is short, pointed, and with the vent close to the shell.

Terrapins are best kept in pairs. However, they do not become sexually mature until they are about five or six years of age.

Accommodation

In its natural warm environment, the terrapin lives on the edge of ponds and rivers, and in freshwater marshes. Always it must have access to water but, at the same time, be able to climb onto rocks and stones so it may bask in the sun.

However, it must be realised that if these creatures are kept in a pond they will attack goldfish and other pond fish, and that they are adept climbers, able to escape from the average pool with the greatest of ease. In Britain, only the European and Spanish Terrapins are hardy enough to survive out of doors throughout the year, when their pond should be netted over and a place provided where the inhabitants can shelter from extremes of temperature.

Small terrapins must be kept indoors, and are easily accommodated in a glass-sided tank, the size of which must depend on the size of the occupants. It should, however, measure at least 38 cm (15 in) in length, and 26 cm (10 in) in width and height. It should be set up in the following way.

Three pieces of rock, two of them supporting the third, will provide a dry area out of the water, and a retreat in the water; the lower surface of the third piece should be about 2 — 3 cm (1 in) above the water allowing the terrapin to surface beneath it. A further piece of rock suitably placed against the others will facilitate access from the water. A piece of curved bark placed on the rocks will provide a dry retreat.

Very young terrapins require a maximum of 5 cm (2 in) of water, but this may be increased for larger ones.

Gravel and water plants are not recommended as these make the daily change of water a lengthy process. However, potted plants placed on the rocks, or suspended by wire hooks from the side of the tank will make an attractive display, especially if the pots can be disguised with a few stones and a little cement.

Terrapins being cold-blooded, that is unable to maintain a body temperature higher than that of their surroundings, it is necessary if you decide to keep a tropical species to maintain it at a temperature of 26−29°C (80−85°F) if you want it to feed and survive. This means that the water must be warmed by a thermostatically controlled water heater as used in tropical fish tanks.

Terrapins, as I have said, enjoy basking in the sun and providing they have sufficient shelter to which they can retire if it gets too hot, this is beneficial. Although the same benefit cannot be derived from a lamp, it is advisable to place one on the lid of the aquarium, or to suspend it above the tank, as they will enjoy the warmth.

Small European terrapins will be content with the heat from the lamp during the summer months, but in winter the heater should be used.

Hibernating

Terrapins may be hibernated in a similar way to land tortoises, but in this case the insulating material must be kept moist during the hibernating period. If the pond in which they are kept is of reasonable depth they may hibernate in the mud at the bottom, but winter in Britain or parts of the United States may be too severe for this method. If, however, these creatures are kept in heated conditions during the winter, they may remain active and feed the whole year round without ill effect.

Feeding

Terrapins are flesh eaters, their pond diet consisting of raw fish, meat and worms as well as tadpoles, small goldfish and other pond life.

The reason, in fact, why so many terrapins die in captivity is because of the inadequacy of the diet, which should include fresh raw fish, especially herrings, fresh raw steak, or other meat, fresh raw liver and kidney, supplemented by watercress and lettuce, powdered cuttlefish bone, or sterilised bonemeal, rubbed into meat daily, and fresh fruit. Proprietary turtle food is not recommended.

Do make sure that any uneaten food is removed each day and that the aquarium is thoroughly cleaned out, and reheated to the previous temperature.

It must be emphasised that daily cleaning obviates the risk of *Salmonella*. However, it is important to encourage children to wash their hands after handling terrapins or other reptiles.

Some people have an aversion to seeing their pets devouring a mouse. Nonetheless it is advisable that a whole mouse or some tinned dog or cat food should be provided once a week. For three terrapins, an adequate quantity of food would be a heaped tablespoonful of tinned cat food, broken into separate bits. If, on the other hand, a mouse is to be fed, the skin should be ripped open so that there is some smell of muscle meat, and if there is likely to be fighting among the terrapins, the offering should be cut, bearing in mind that one of them will go for, and obtain, the liver. It is a case of the survival of the fittest—the best gets the liver.

There is a high incidence of calcium deficiency and soft shell disease in terrapins due entirely to the wrong diet being provided, a diet given all too often because the purchaser was recommended to buy 'turtle' food, which is totally unbalanced.

Breeding and care of young

Terrapins become sexually mature at five or six years of age when, if eggs are produced they should be placed in a polythene bag containing loose, damp sand (or soil) and incubated at 29°C (85°F), hatching taking place in approximately three to five months.

The young specimens are more successfully kept indoors in the winter at a summer temperature of 24°—27°C (75°—80°F) and fed as usual. On dull days an electric lamp over their tank will help to keep them active.

If rain water can be procured this is more satisfactory as 'hard' town water appears to be detrimental to the eyes of some specimens.

Minnows are a useful food for young terrapins and fishermen should be able to catch them with ease; whitebait and cut up bits of herrings and sprats are also suitable and, while fresh raw liver is a diet which should not be encouraged in excess, it is a good source of natural Vitamin A and when taken by mouth will do more good than when injected, although treatment for a gross Vitamin A deficiency must be started by injections from a veterinary surgeon.

Ailments

Soft shell: Most diseases in terrapins would appear to come about through incorrect feeding and lack of calcium, particularly soft shell, recovery from which may be possible if given veterinary care coupled with a diet of whole young herrings, sprats, shrimps, insects and water snails supplemented by sterilised bone meal rubbed into the food. However, once little terrapins, and not necessarily the very tiniest creatures but those of 8—10 cm (3—4 in) in length, have been fed an incorrect diet, they are incapable of growing a decent shell and will be deformed for the rest of their lives.

Eyes: Eye trouble can also result from faulty feeding, another cause being foul water which, if not changed immediately, may cause blindness. Rain water has been found to be more beneficial than hard town water to the eyes.

Bathe the eyes several times a day with cotton wool soaked in a warm, weak solution of boracic acid or salt.

Food refusal: If the terrapin refuses food this could be because it is being kept at too low a temperature and this should be raised immediately to 26°—29°C (80°—85°F).

Other problems include worms, fungal infections and skin shedding. Shedding is a natural process and fragments should not be removed by the owner. Fungus, however, is something quite different and can often be cleared by applying a strong salt solution.

There is no cause for concern if a green growth appears on the shell. This is a growth of microscopic plants or algae and is a normal occurrence.

Remember that a chelonian should be able to lift its body off the ground. A very healthy one can turn itself over rapidly.

6
Lizards

Lizards, which so often seem to resemble dragons in miniature, can be as small as 5 cm (2 in) or as large as 3 m (10 ft) in length. They make fascinating pets, but be warned that their lifespan is shorter than other reptiles and, unlike many snakes which can, with good husbandry, live in captivity for twenty years or more, the lizard often survives for only five years or less.

Type, general information and sexing

There are more lizards than any other type of reptile and, with the exception of the polar regions, their distribution is worldwide. You are, however, more likely to see them basking in the sun on a tropical verandah.

The typical lizard, though there are many exceptions, has four legs, five toes on each foot, and a sprawling gait, presenting a study in miniature of the ancient reptiles that once roamed the earth. Characteristics of the lizard are that it has eyelids, so can close its eyes, and has external ears so can hear airborne sounds. It sheds its skin once a month, sloughing it off in patches, or a scale at a time. It is clean, odourless and fascinating to keep, although some varieties are more attractive to look at than others. Most varieties adore spiders and an offer of this delicacy goes a long way towards taming them.

Most lizards have an unforked tongue with which they pick up tastes and swallow food. Sometimes a gecko will use its tongue like a windscreen wiper across its eyes while a chameleon uses its tongue to shoot and haul in its prey. Its tongue is three-quarters the length of its body, and it is most adept at camouflaging itself to merge in colour with its surroundings.

It is usual for the male of the species to have a thicker tail than the female though this is by no means always the case (see Figure 22). Again, most lay eggs but some are live bearers and an interesting point is that while some lizards refuse to drink from a dish they will always accept drops from a leaf.

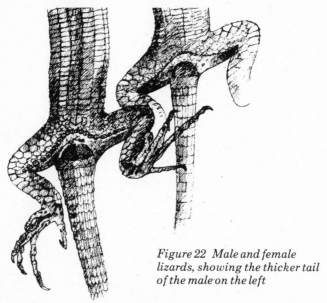

Figure 22 Male and female lizards, showing the thicker tail of the male on the left

In the wild in Britain, one is most likely to find the Common Lizard—which is a live bearer—on arid land such as heaths and commons. Usually it is olive brown in colour with a broken line down its back and it has an orange under-side, spotted black in the male, and grey in the female; it is very lively. Common in Britain also is the Slow Worm, which is a legless lizard and grows to about 45 cm (18 in). Our third species, the Sand Lizard, is found in only a few scattered localities.

Other parts of the world are much better endowed with lizards of varying types. All in all there are thirteen families: the geckos; the night lizards; the iguanas which include the horned lizards; the agamas; the chameleons; the skinks; the zonures; the plated lizards; the lacertids which include the Eyed Lizard, the Green Lizard and the Wall Lizard; the tegus and whiptails or racerunners; the anguids among which are found slow worms, glass lizards and alligator lizards; the monitors, known primarily for the Komodo Dragon which is the largest of all lizards; and finally there is the rather obscure family of the amphisbaenians, burrowing reptiles which are most unlikely to turn up in captivity.

So which type of lizard should you choose? The many species of gecko are amiable house prowlers which eat insects in house plants; but most are delicate and readily shed their tails when handled, so they should be kept in a safe place. Incidentally, although the majority of lizards, those for instance with a long, low body, short legs and a long tail, were designed for running on the ground, most geckos have toe pads, with fine hairs, that grip a smooth surface and enable them even to run along a ceiling.

Figure 23 Kotschy's Gecko, Cyrtodactylus kotschyi, *found in arid parts of southern Europe*

Chameleons are one of the most popular lizard varieties to keep as a pet, but they are delicate and not unreservedly recommended to the beginner. It is unnecessary to keep a chameleon confined and it will thrive in any warm, sunny atmosphere. However, if, as is likely, a vivarium is to be used, a few twigs are absolutely essential. Chameleons rarely breed in captivity and one of the sad facts of ownership is that under closely confined conditions they rarely survive more than a matter of months while a sudden light and colourful change of hue can be an indication of fast approaching death.

Figure 24 Kuhl's Gecko, Ptychozoon kuhli, *shown here eating a crane fly*

Horned lizards, of which there are about 12 species, skinks which comprise a very large family, plated lizards and racerunners or whip-tails can be found in varying sizes and make good pets, as will several other varieties stocked by your pet shop. Seek advice on which ones you put together though, as some of the larger species could eat the smaller ones. Refer also to the List of Lizards Suited to Captivity on page 57.

Accommodation

The lizard, in common with the snake (Chapter 7), will do well in a glass aquarium, or terrarium, with a well-fastened, ventilated cover. Temperature and humidity are easily controlled in a home like this, and it can be cleaned with relative ease. Make sure though that you keep the temperature and humidity at the proper level for your pet. This will vary from species to species. While a temperature of around 26°C (82°F) seems to suit many varieties, it is important to check this out at the time of purchase.

Figure 25 Five-lined Skink, Eumeces fasciatus

It should be remembered that lizards will bask for a while each day so as to raise their body temperature to a comfortable level, then they will retreat to a cooler area before they become overheated. It is essential therefore that a lamp is set up to shine on a particular spot as a suitable basking site (see Figure 26), and that the accommodation is big enough for the animal to move far enough away to feed and move around in a cooler area.

Remember to study the natural history of your chosen pet before furnishing and planting its aquarium: if it is a tree dweller you should supply some means of allowing it to climb, and you will have to provide a relatively large, tall vivarium. If the pet is used to having water nearby, this will have to be provided in the form of a combined aquarium/vivarium.

The Horned Lizard of the American West likes to bury himself in the sand; other lizards are similarly shy and enjoy the privacy of rocks, or small logs which can be arranged as a retreat and a large upside down flower pot with a hole in it makes a perfect hiding place.

Figure 26 In this vivarium, a lamp shines on a suitable basking spot but the accommodation is big enough to allow retreat to a cooler area

Feeding

The larger types of lizard eat mammals and birds and will benefit from canned dog food in addition to fruit. Some enjoy earthworms, mealworms, crickets and even cockroaches and all seem to adore spiders. And although fruit and vegetables are so enjoyed, particularly by iguanas, multivitamins and powdered cuttlefish bone should be offered.

Lizards vary from relatively tiny creatures such as small geckos up through the larger varieties to water dragons and iguanas, some people keeping skinks, some chameleons and others Slow Worms. The aim must always be to feed the right diet bearing in mind that, in captivity, it is unlikely that it will be receiving the same rations as it would in the wild.

The majority of lizards are insectivorous and will like mealworms. However, a mealworm by itself—because we are keeping it, and breeding it, in bran—contains the wrong mineral content; it is the correct mineral content for breeding mealworms, but the wrong mineral content for absorption by lizards. Because of this, it is necessary for the insect being used as food to be fed on a diet which has sufficient extra calcium, minerals and vitamins, for these to be in the intestine of the insect when it is eaten as prey. If, for example, the lizard owner merely feeds mealworms straight from the bran pot, they will indeed be consumed by the lizard, but within a year the pet will be suffering from calcium malnutrition (see Diseases, below).

Indeed, the calcium problem in large lizards and iguanas is so great that expert Dr Oliphant Jackson recommends feeding them on tinned dog or cat food which has been fortified with vitamins and minerals intended for the growth of puppies and kittens. Feeding of whole small mice is also advocated.

Figure 27 Curly-tailed Iguana, Leiocephalus barahonensis. *This species, attaining a length of some 30 cm (12 in) is not unreservedly recommended to the beginner as it needs a large vivarium and a consistently high temperature*

Incidentally, an advantage in keeping some types of lizard, such as the gecko, is that one can gauge their fitness in that they put their food reserves into their tail. The creature with a tail that is thinner than its companion will be the one that has not had sufficient food intake.

Diet is all important. Some of the larger lizards, including the iguanas, enjoy vegetables and fruit, but it is essential that owners should realise that, because a lizard likes a particular fruit it should not become its sole diet.

The diet of iguanas should include chopped fruits and vegetables such as pear, cabbage, lettuce, dandelion (including the flower), rose petals, clover leaf and clover flower, bananas on occasions, insects, and tinned dog or cat food (or, of course, a mouse!)

Figure 28 Green Iguana, Iguana iguana. *This is a young specimen in a typical basking position. It is a favourite in zoological gardens but can attain a length of 150 cm (60 in) so is most unsuitable for a domestic environment*

Diseases

The diseases of lizards include mouth rot and snout abrasion, conditions which call for treatment with antibiotics by a veterinarian. Abscesses should also be treated by a veterinarian. Calcium deficiency is a common complaint for which you can look for a number of symptoms. First of all, the lizard will not walk up on its legs as it should do. A healthy lizard is perpetually up on its legs, able to take its weight on them, with the body raised off. Indeed, the moment you have a creature which is calcium deficient, it will appear flat, unable to lift, and with no strength whatsoever in its legs. The remedy is improved feeding, as outlined under feeding, above, but be vigilant for the signs which could mean the difference between life and death.

One cannot overemphasise the importance of seeking a veterinarian's help whenever there is the slightest doubt as to a pet's health rather than attempting home remedies or deciding that a condition is incurable in the absence of professional diagnosis. For instance, a limb may be successfully put in a plaster cast and amputations may be effected where a tumour or gangrenous condition demands it. In such circumstances the lizard may well continue to be mobile using its tail as a balancing aid.

Figure 29 Leopard Gecko, Eublepharus macularius

Figure 30 Green Anole, Anolis carolinensis

Figure 31 Wall Lizard, Podarcis muralis

List of Lizards Suited to Captivity

N.B. The temperatures given are averages of the basking site and the rest of the vivarium. Remember to provide a temperature gradient for all lizards varying about 3°C (5°F) either side of the stated temperature.

Geckos

Gonatodes species 7 cm (3 in)
Tall vivarium, 20°C (68°F), well planted and with branches for climbing; feed small insects including flies.

Turkish Gecko 9 cm (4 in)
Hemidactylus turcicus
Vivarium, 26°C (80°F) with stony ground, but facility for climbing and hiding; feed small insects.

Banded Gecko 10 cm (4 in)
Coleonyx variegatus
Vivarium, 25°C (77°F), with stony ground; feed small insects, larvae and mealworms.

Day Gecko 12 cm (5 in)
Phelsuma cepediana
Vivarium, 26°C (80°F), well-planted for hiding places and with gravelly ground; feed insects including flies.

Flat-tailed Day Gecko 12 cm (5 in)
Phelsuma laticauda
Vivarium, 26°C (80°F), planted thickly and with gravelly ground; feed insects including flies.

Kuhl's Gecko 17 cm (7 in)
Ptychozoon kuhli
(See Figure 24)
Vivarium, 26°C (80°F), with branches for climbing, and stony ground; feed large insects.

Leopard Gecko 22 cm (9 in)
Eublepharus macularius
(See Figure 29)
Vivarium, 27°C (80°F), with stony ground or newspaper or sand and hiding places; feed insects, larvae and mealworms.

Tokay Gecko 33 cm (13 in)
Gekko gecko
Large vivarium, 27°C (80°F), with stony ground and hiding places; feed large insects and small pieces of meat.

Iguanas

Green Anole 12 cm (5 in)
Anolis carolinensis
(See Figure 30)

Large, tall, vivarium, 26°C (80°F), with gravelly ground and branches for climbing; feed insects particularly flies and provide water by spraying foliage regularly.

Brown Anole 12 cm (5 in)
Anolis sagrei

Large vivarium, 26°C (80°F), with gravelly ground and branches; feed insects and provide water by spraying foliage regularly.

Western Fence Lizard
13 cm (5 in)
Sceloporus occidentalis

Large vivarium, 26°C (80°F), with rocks and logs; feed insects.

Horned Lizards 15 cm (6 in)
Phrynosoma spp.

Large vivarium, 30°C (86°F), with gravel or sand ground; feed ants, other small insects and larvae, pieces of meat and some vegetable matter.

Skinks

Five-lined Skink 12 cm (5 in)
Eumeces fasciatus
(See Figure 25)

Vivarium, 25°C (77°F), with patches of moist and dry ground; feed insects.

Western Skink 12 cm (5 in)
Eumeces skiltonianus

Vivarium, 25°C (77°F), with mossy ground and islands of sand; feed insects.

African Five-lined Skink
20 cm (8 in)
Mabuya quinquetaeniatus

Vivarium, 25°C (77°F), with leafy or mossy ground and patches of dry ground; feed insects and pieces of fruit.

Lined Skink 30 cm (12 in)
Chalcides chalcides

Vivarium, 25°C (77°F), with mossy ground, and patches of moisture; feed fruit, pieces of meat and insects.

Blue-tongued Skink 50 cm (20 in)
Tiliqua gigas

Large vivarium, 25°C (77°F), with logs for hiding, and a ground of leaves and moss; feed small pieces of meat, insects, fruit and vegetables.

Figure 32 Green Lizard, Lacerta viridis

Figure 33 European Agama, Agama stellio

Zonures

Jones' Zonure 12 cm (5 in)
Cordylus jonesi

Large vivarium, 32°C (90°F), with gravel or newspaper ground and rocks for basking and hiding; feed insects and small pieces of meat.

Rock Lizard 25 cm (10 in)
Pseudocordylus subviridis

Very large vivarium, 32°C (90°F), with rocks for basking, the rest of the cage lined with newspaper or gravel; feed insects and small pieces of meat.

Racerunners

Six-lined Racerunner 20 cm (8 in)
Cnemidophorus sexlineatus

Large, dry vivarium, 30°C (86°F) with gravel or sand ground and rocks for basking and hiding beneath; feed insects.

Chameleons

African Chameleon 20 cm (8 in)
Chamaeleo bitaeniatus

Vivarium, 27°C (82°F), with branches for climbing; feed insects, and provide water by spraying foliage.

Flap-necked Chameleon 30 cm (12 in)
Chamaeleo dilepis

Vivarium or greenhouse, 27°C (82°F), with branches for climbing; feed insects and provide water by spraying foliage.

Jackson's Chameleon 40 cm (16 in)
Chamaeleo jacksoni

Large vivarium or greenhouse, 27°C (82°F), well planted and with branches for climbing; feed insects and larvae, and provide water by spraying foliage.

Lacertids

Wall Lizard 20 cm (8 in)
Podarcis muralis
(See Figure 31)

Large vivarium, 25°C (77°F), with gravelly ground, and rocks and logs for climbing and hiding; feed insects including flies.

Ruin Lizard 20 cm (8 in)
Podarcis sicula

Large vivarium, 26°C (80°F), with rocky and gravelly ground; feed insects including flies.

Green Lizard 35 cm (14 in) *Lacerta viridis* (See Figure 32)	Very large vivarium or greenhouse, 26°C (80°F), planted and with rocks and branches; feed large insects, some fruit and greenfood and small pieces of meat, provide water by spraying foliage.
Eyed Lizard 60 cm (24 in) *Lacerta lepida*	Very large vivarium or greenhouse, 26°C (80°F), planted and with branches for climbing; feed large insects and some fruit; provide water by spraying foliage.

Agamas

Agamas 30 cm (12 in) *Agama* spp. (See Figure 33)	Large vivarium, 28°C (82°F), gravelly ground with rocks and logs for hiding places and basking; feed insects and some fruit; provide drinking water by spraying foliage.

Plated Lizards

Yellow-throated Plated Lizard 40 cm (16 in) *Gerrhosaurus flavigularis*	Very large vivarium, 32°C (90°F), with rocks for basking and hiding, gravel or newspaper ground; feed insects, mice, pieces of meat.

Anguids

Northern Alligator Lizard 30 cm (12 in) *Gerrhonotus coeruleus*	Large, moist vivarium, 22°C (72°F), well planted and with mossy ground with rocks and branches; feed insects and larvae.
Southern Alligator Lizard 30 cm (12 in) *Gerrhonotus multicarinatus*	Moist vivarium, 22°C (72°F), well-planted and with ferns and moss, with some rocks and branches; feed insects and larvae.
Slow Worm 40 cm (16 in) *Anguis fragilis*	Moist vivarium, 19°C (67°F), with shade and hiding places among moss, bark, ferns; feed insects and larvae.
Glass-snake 100 cm (40 in) *Ophisaurus apodus*	Very large vivarium, 27°C (80°F), with newspaper and pieces of branch and rock; feed large insects and larvae and small pieces of meat.

7
Snakes

Snakes, though feared in many quarters, have a fascination which has compelled man since time immemorial, since the Garden of Eden, in fact. They have been associated with everything from black magic and witch doctors to fertility; they have been the accessories of stage artistes and flute-playing charmers and have featured in Greek mythology. They are still believed by many to have supernatural powers and the gift of healing. Indeed the Aesculapian snake, (*Elaphe longissima*), was believed to be the serpent on the symbol of Aesculapius the Greek god of medicine, and in the temple of Aesculapius in Epidaurus, Greece, the god's reputed birthplace, large amiable snakes have been identified as of this type and thought to be incarnations of the god with healing powers.

The snake is a reptile differing in many respects from the lizard: it is without moveable eyelids or external ears and varies in size from as little as 12 cm (5 in) to as long as 9 m (30 ft). Because its eyes are perpetually open, the snake always appears to be staring at its observer while, despite its lack of external ears, it can hear, or rather sense, vibrations through its skull bones.

It has a forked tongue which functions as both scent and taste organ and darts in and out enabling the snake to sample the air. In fact, it is a unique smelling-tasting tool which enables the snake to follow its prey, sample food, locate a mate, or simply warn away its enemies.

Snakes have a single row of scales underneath that help them to move much like the tread of a tractor. They do not shed their tails and grow new ones as lizards do, but they do shed their skins all in one piece from head to foot, leaving behind a cellophane-like wrapper when they emerge. If pieces of skin stick to your captive snake, you should fold it in a damp cloth for some hours after which you should be able to pull off the offending bits with tweezers.

Figure 34 Red-sided Garter Snake, Thamnophis sirtalis parietalis

Accommodation

The most secure place for your pet is a glass aquarium or terrarium with a well-fastened, ventilated cover. (You should be able to see and/or buy examples at your pet stores but refer also to Chapter 1). The lid should, preferably, have small holes drilled in it, or a section of it be fitted with perforated zinc to provide ventilation. Or the vivarium can be made of wood, and glass fronted. It can be furnished to reproduce the natural environment of your pet, whether woodland or meadow.

The floor of the vivarium should be covered with large gravel, plastic foam or paper, but not soil, peat, sand or sawdust. A curved piece of bark, or a cave made of pieces of stone, should be provided so that the snake can hide when it wishes. A dish, half full of water, is essential since snakes drink water frequently and the Dice Snake,

Grass Snake and Garter Snake sometimes bathe in it. Plastic plants and branches may also be included. But remember that the sides, floor and furnishings must be washed every few weeks. The enclosure should be positioned out of direct sunlight.

There is, of course, no objection to keeping reptile pets on fresh paper. This is what is used in pet shops. It is cheap and unlikely to cause harm. Paper tissue is recommended in that it allows easy cleaning, the vivarium lid being removed simply, the water dish being set aside, and the soiled paper being discarded.

A small 40−60 watt light bulb should be fitted in the vivarium top to provide light and heat during the day, making sure, by means of a thermometer that the temperature reaches 24°−27°C (75°−80°F). If you live in a centrally heated house no heat will be required at night. However, if the room where you have the snake is a cold one, it is best to heat the vivarium at night also. A low wattage bulb, painted black, should keep the temperature at around 18°−21°C (65°−70°F) and a thermostat can be used to regulate this.

Figure 35 Western Ribbon Snake, Thamnophis proximus. *The Eastern and Western Ribbon Snakes require similar care in captivity to the garter snakes*

Essentials are cleanliness, security, ventilation and, of course, heating and lighting. It cannot be over-emphasised that the vivarium *must* be kept clean. Large droppings should be removed whilst fresh and the entire vivarium, and all its furnishings, cleaned every 2−3 weeks depending on the extent of the fouling. A chlorine based disinfectant such as 'Milton' is suitable.

It is also vital that the vivarium be escape proof. A snake is not incapable of getting out of its tank by pushing its nose against the nylon mesh and making a hole in it. Indeed it is a good idea to keep a snake in a box within a larger vivarium. If a snake disappears, the survival chances of some species are obviously greater than others, those tolerant of low temperatures enjoying a higher survival rate. Preferred temperatures are given in the List of Snakes Suited to Captivity on page 68.

This 'preferred' temperature is that at which the reptiles like to live. Indeed if one produced a lengthy vivarium with the higher range at one end and the cooler at the other, it would be noted that the snake

Figure 36 Green Water Snake, Nerodia cyclopion

would move along the gradient at different times of the day and night.

The digestive enzymes, which are secreted by the stomach for food digestion, can act only at these preferred temperatures. Therefore, if you maintain a reptile at a very cold temperature, it will be unable to digest its food, although it may continue to eat.

Feeding

Snakes are able to consume live food which is bigger than they are, because their heads and jaws are designed for it. They have very specialised diets and their digestive systems allow them to wait until the right meal turns up—two weeks or even a month. In captivity snakes still crave their favourite food, be it mice, baby chickens, frogs, worms or salamanders. But, if you are patient, some may eat non live food such as raw fish or raw meat, particularly if you wiggle it to make the snake think the offering is alive. Be sure to learn the feeding habits of your snake and remember not to handle it after feeding. It needs time to digest its food.

The frequency of feeding must vary from species to species, and you should refer to the List of Snakes Suited to Captivity on page 68 for details. Remember in general, however, that in the period of approximately 10 days before it sloughs its skin it is unlikely to feed. At that time, the snake will be feeling somewhat uncomfortable, its eyes, as I indicated earlier, will become cloudy, there will be a milky appearance separating the old skin from the new, and it will not want to constrict. Indeed, it will, in all probability, go into hiding.

Remember that if you overfeed a snake you are going to have a fat one and, in consequence, its liver will become over fat and you will run into trouble. Don't starve your snake but do keep it reasonably slim.

When a snake kills its prey, and it will kill only when it is hungry, everything is digested: the skin, the skeleton, the liver, the intestinal contents, everything except hair, horn or hoof, all of which is excreted, the hair coming out like a mat of felt which is why, with a rodent-eating snake, one uses the term 'felt' instead of faeces.

Going up the scale, a really large snake will consume a chicken or a rabbit whole and, in the wild, when large pythons take a Bush Buck or Impala, it will last them for approximately six months.

If you keep several snakes together, separate them at feeding time, otherwise, in their enthusiasm, more than one snake may grab the

same food, they will be reluctant to let go and one snake may swallow
another.

Diseases

Slough failure

If the skin comes off piecemeal, which it should not do, except in the
case of gigantic snakes, this is an indication that something is amiss
with the humidity. The owner must question the cause. Quite likely it
could be that the vivarium has been placed on a radiator which, while
producing warmth, is also carrying off all the moisture.

Colds and pneumonia

Veterinary assistance should be sought. The patient will need antibiotics and isolation at 30°C (86°F).

Ticks

These can be exterminated with kerosine and thereafter removed
with tweezers.

Mouth rot and skin abrasion

This condition needs treatment with antibiotics. Isolate the patient
and consult a vet.

It is not uncommon for snakes to suffer from scale rot (blister
disease) which, in fact, is a bacterial infection. The first sign of skin
disease is an abnormal appearance of the skin. But with a snake the
signal that all is not well is in its feeding pattern, which becomes
irregular. Veterinary help must be sought.

Much is now being done to help the veterinarian in general practice
to treat reptilian pets. Indeed, over the last 10 years, Dr Oliphant
Jackson and his associate, John Cooper, have been lecturing to
veterinary groups in Britain, showing pictures of reptile diseases,
telling their audiences how to arrive at a diagnosis and advocating
treatment. They have also produced a tape/slide programme, which is
available through the Royal Veterinary College in Camden Town,
London, and a section on reptiles, 'Children's Exotic Pets', has been
contributed by Dr Jackson to the *Veterinarian's Manual* thus
ensuring that the owner of a snake—and indeed lizard or
chelonian—will receive as much care as the owner of a more widely
kept dog or cat when visiting the surgery.

List of Snakes Suited to Captivity

As the basic requirements of most snakes are very similar the only details given here are for specific preferences. For general information refer to the sections on accommodation and feeding, above.

Blind Snakes

Typhlops spp. 20−70 cm (8−28 in)

Unusual in needing deep sandy soil for burrowing, keep at about 26°C (78°F); feed soil dwelling invertebrates.

Colubrids

Dice Snake 60 cm (24 in)
Natrix tessellata

Newspaper or bark ground with gravel or rock for basking, 25°C (77°F); feed raw fish and whitebait.

Plains Garter Snake 75 cm (30 in)
Thamnophis radix

Dry leaves, newspaper or bark ground with pots and branches for cover, 24°C (75°F); feed whole raw fish, and also earthworms, slugs and small pieces of meat.

Chequered Garter Snake 75 cm (30 in)
Thamnophis marcianus

Newspaper ground with gravel for basking and rocks and pots for cover, 24°C (75°F); feed whole raw fish including whitebait, and earthworms, slugs and small pieces meat.

Common garter snakes 50−120 cm (20−48 in)
Thamnophis sirtalis subspp.
(See Figures 34 and 35)

Newspaper ground with gravel for basking and rocks for cover, 24°C (75°F); feed whole fish, mice, earthworms, slugs and pieces of meat.

Tricoloured Kingsnake 75 cm (30 in)
Lampropeltis pyromelana

Newspaper, dry leaves or bark ground, 27°C (80°F) with branches and rocks for cover; keep alone; feed rodents.

Leopard Snake 80 cm (32 in)
Elaphe situla

Tall vivarium with branches for climbing and cover, 27°C (80°F), with newspaper or dry leaves ground; feed rodents.

Figure 37 Corn Snake, Elaphe guttata

Figure 38 Four-lined Snake, Elaphe quatuorlineata

Grass Snake 90 cm (36 in)
Natrix natrix

Newspaper or bark ground with gravel for basking, 25°C (77°F); feed whole raw fish including whitebait.

Water snakes 90 cm (36 in)
Nerodia spp.
(See Figure 36)

Newspaper ground with gravel for basking away from water source, 27°C (80°F); feed whole raw fish.

Prairie Kingsnake 100 cm (40 in)
Lampropeltis calligaster

Newspaper, bark or dry leaves ground, with branches or pots for cover, 26°C (78°F); keep alone; feed rodents.

Glossy Snake 100 cm (40 in)
Arizona elegans

Newspaper ground with rock for basking, 27°C (80°F); feed small mice, or small lizards if possible.

House Snake 100 cm (40 in)
Boaedon fuliginosus

Newspaper or bark ground with gravel or rock for basking, 26°C (78°F); feed small mice.

Western Whipsnake 125 cm (50 in)
Coluber viridiflavus

Newspaper or dry leaves with rock for basking, 25°C (77°F); feed small mice, or small lizards if possible, and earthworms, slugs and larvae.

Corn Snake 125 cm (50 in)
Elaphe guttata
(See Figure 37)

Tall vivarium, 27°C (80°F), with branches for climbing and for cover, with newspaper ground; feed rodents or small lizards if possible.

Aesculapian Snake 125 cm (50 in)
Elaphe longissima

Tall vivarium, 27°C (80°F), with branches for climbing and for cover, with newspaper ground; feed rodents, or small lizards if possible.

Common kingsnakes 140 cm (56 in)
Lampropeltis getulus
subspp.

Newspaper, bark or dry leaves ground with branches or pots for cover, 26°C (78°F); keep alone; feed rodents.

Four-lined Snake 160 cm (64 in)
Elaphe quatuorlineata
(See Figure 38)

Tall vivarium, 27°C (80°F), with branches for climbing and cover, with newspaper or dry leaves ground; feed rodents or small lizards.

Mole Snake 160 cm (64 in) *Pseudaspis cana*	Newspaper, bark and dry leaves ground with rocks and branches for basking and cover, 27°C (80°F); feed rodents.
Rat snakes 175 cm (70 in) *Elaphe obsoleta* subspp.	Tall vivarium, 27°C (80°F), with branches for climbing and for cover, with newspaper ground; feed rodents.
Asian Rat Snake 175 cm (70 in) *Ptyas mucosus*	Tall vivarium, 27°C (80°F), with branches for climbing and cover, with newspaper ground; feed rodents.

Boas

Sand Boa 70 cm (28 in) *Eryx jaculus*	27°C (80°F) gravel with stones for burrowing under; feed rats, mice and dead birds.
Royal Python 150 cm (60 in) *Python regius*	Newspaper ground, 27°C (80°F), with bark and branches; feed rodents.
Rainbow Boa 200 cm (80 in) *Epicrates cenchria*	Tall vivarium, 27°C (80°F), with branches for climbing, newspaper ground; feed rodents, chickens.
Boa Constrictor 300 cm (120 in) *Boa constrictor*	Provide branches in a tall vivarium, 27°C (80°F), with newspaper ground; feed rodents, chickens.
Indian Python 600 cm (240 in) *Python molurus*	Few people will be able to provide large enough accommodation for this huge snake, though they make good subjects; 27°C (80°F), newspaper ground, with bark and branches; feed rodents, chickens.

8
Recording and conserving in the wild

Reptiles and amphibians, along with many other classes of animal, are suffering in many parts of the world because of destruction of their habitat. There has also been a significant decrease in the populations of some species, not only because of malicious treatment, but also because of the collection of individuals, not for captive-breeding programmes but to be kept in isolation.

This book aims to help the beginner to learn about reptiles and amphibians, and in the first instance to care properly for individuals. It is to be hoped, however, that the eventual aim of all herpetologists should be to breed from their captive animals, supplying the needs of other hobbyists, so that wild populations need not be depleted. It is the case that the wild populations of some few species of endangered animal have been augmented by captive-bred stock, and this is perhaps the ultimate aim that the herpetologist can aspire to.

There are two international conventions of which the conservation-minded hobbyist should be aware. These are CITES—The Convention on International Trade in Endangered Species—and The Convention on the Conservation of European Wildlife and Natural Habitats. Under the latter all European reptiles and amphibians are listed as protected species except those which have strictly protected status. Britain is not in fact a party to either Convention, but four of its twelve species of native reptiles and amphibians are protected under the Wildlife and Countryside Act of 1981. These are the Crested Newt, the Natterjack Toad, the Sand Lizard and the Smooth Snake.

It is stressed throughout this book that a knowledge of the natural history of a species is essential to a thorough understanding of how it will prosper in captivity. An interest in the local populations of frogs, toads and snakes, if resulting in careful recording of observations, can also be of tremendous use to the professional biologist. The following account of the status of reptiles and amphibians in Britain, and the help which amateurs can afford to biologists should give an idea of schemes which could be set up locally worldwide to the benefit of this group of animals.

In Britain there are three species of lizards (Common or Viviparous Lizard, Sand Lizard and Slow Worm or Blind Worm), three species of snakes (the Grass or Ringed Snake, Adder or Northern Viper and Smooth Snake),three species of newts (the Common or Smooth Newt, Warty or Great Crested Newt and Palmate Newt) and three species of frogs and toads (the Common Frog, Common Toad, and Natterjack Toad), but, while chances of seeing some of these were always remote, the species were, in the past, thriving. Today, even the Common Frog has ceased to be a familiar sight and numbers of other species are decreasing alarmingly, the four protected species listed above being almost threatened with extinction.

The RSPCA suggests three main causes for the depleting numbers: first and foremost the destruction of the animals' natural habitat as ponds, streams and other waterways are drained, or fall into disuse, thus depriving amphibians of the necessary environment in which to lay eggs, or in which their tadpoles may develop, while, with urbanisation and the growth of agriculture, much of the sandy heathland of southern England has been lost, leading to the disappearance of Sand Lizards, Natterjack Toads and Smooth Snakes whose numbers were never plentiful.

Secondly, there is the destructive element of man polluting ponds, streams and other waterways bearing in mind that, while local authorities face up to their responsibilities in avoiding and eliminating direct chemical pollution to their waterways, they have little control over pesticides, used for crop protection, which drain off fields and contaminate local waters. Often such pesticides are used carelessly with little thought as to the damage they will do to nearby water-life.

Thirdly, and importantly,there is the threat of indiscriminate collectors, the thoughtless wildlife enthusiasts who, in their eagerness to obtain a certain species, will plunder it from an area in which its numbers are already far too few

And yet no one would wish to dissuade any well-intentioned collector from pursuing their hobby and it was with this point in mind that I paid a visit to the Biological Records Centre in Huntingdonshire where records are kept of the distribution of amphibians and reptiles throughout the British Isles, a centre where I was happy to find evidence of real concern for the continuance of the life-cycle of friends such as the Common Frog and Common Toad, and to learn how caring people can help to assure that these creatures remain as part of our wild life.

At the Records Centre I discovered that there are certain problems in keeping frogs and toads as pets. It is, for instance, discouraging and negative to say to children that they must not go and collect a jar of frog spawn. Yet if it is collected by the jarful there is bound to be a high mortality rate, unless the collector has a large aquarium, because, where you have a whole clump of spawn, there is a potential of something like 2,000 tadpoles. What the collector needs is a reasonably sized aquarium and — rather than a whole clump of spawn — simply part of it.

Tadpoles, of course, need feeding, initially on tinned spinach and boiled lettuce, and once the hind legs start developing, on meat and on scraps of bone with meat attached, taking care that food is not left in the aquarium too long, or it will start to decay.

The collector must also realise that young frogs, just as they start to emerge, can drown quite easily. So either they should be released — just as the front legs begin to appear — back into the pond from which they came, or into a suitable garden pond. Otherwise, immense care must be taken to ensure that there are stones and suchlike in the aquarium that the frogs can climb onto. They will, in any case, need to be released before they start hopping around.

Never release frogs into running water. You do sometimes get frog spawn in slow flowing streams, but not often. The best pond for frogs is the clean, natural pond with plenty of vegetation and not too many fish. Goldfish in a garden pond are liable to gobble up tadpoles. And you must also expect a high mortality rate if there are large numbers of water beetles.

If you can rear tadpoles to the stage where their front legs are beginning to appear and return them to the pond when they are too large for the water beetle, you should successfully increase the population.

At the Biological Records Centre a data bank is being set up which records the distribution of flowers and wildlife in the United Kingdom, such information being available to all research workers and conservationists. National societies are encouraged to organise a recording scheme, the Records Centre providing record cards and advice on how to maintain them.

The fond hope is that scheme organisers will run a scheme for five or ten years, whatever period they think necessary, and when sufficient information has been collected, that they should send the data, which will have been neatly written out, and checked, to the Centre. The findings will be fed into the computer becoming part of the data bank and help to produce distribution maps.

Surprisingly perhaps, there are more schoolgoers than teachers engaged in this type of research. Where you have an interested schoolmaster he will organise his biology class to go out and make records. But there are more dedicated individuals than organised groups, and there are limitations also as to what the average ten-year-old can do by way of detection. He can probably be trusted to identify frogs and toads correctly, but newts, for instance, provide a greater challenge, particularly outside the breeding season.

Advice to collectors from the Biological Records Centre is to choose an area around their home and record it in detail. Such an assignment depends to some extent on their mobility and age. However, they may like to record where all the ponds are in their district—farm ponds and ditches, places where there are likely to be frogs and toads —discovering all the breeding sites and how successful they are by, for example, finding out if they dry up during the summer when there might be a high tadpole mortality rate.

If you cannot cover the usual distribution area which is 10 km (6¾ miles) square, you can at least have a go at recording what is happening to the environment. Record when ponds disappear, speak to elderly local people who may remember the sites of ponds which once harboured frogs and toads in large numbers, and write, if you like, a report of how things once were, and the way they have now become. Such information could prove a great assistance to the Centre.

If you can, make a pond in your own garden and above all keep your eyes and ears open, because if a pond is to be filled in, a shout in the right direction could possibly save it.

Establishing a garden pond is simple. You can buy preformed polystyrene pools, or use a polythene sheet. If you choose the latter, and if you buy the heavy duty polythene sheet, the Records Centre can help with instructions. Basically, however, you dig out the hole remembering to dig so that there are various water levels, 60—90 cm (2—3 ft) deep for toads, about 45 cm (18 in) deep for frogs. You must have shallow areas, and routes out of the pond, so that the tadpoles can get out if they wish. Line the hole with very fine sand or wet newspapers, something to prevent the stones coming through and piercing the polythene. Then you just lay it down weighing it round the edges with rocks, or paving slabs, and, if you leave gaps in between the rocks, so that there are nooks and crannies for the tadpoles, make sure that these are nice and moist. It is a good idea to have some fairly long vegetation nearby, so that the toadlets and froglets can get out into it, and be protected from predators, when they first emerge. Cats may catch the odd frog but this is a rare occurrence rather than a regular hazard.

Do remember not to use pesticide sprays. They would be poisonous to frogs and other wildlife. It is all too easy when spraying the air for the aerosol content to drift over, and into, the pond killing the tadpoles.

Sometimes, if you have dug a garden pond and put vegetation in it, frogs may find their way to it naturally. Indeed, where there are few natural ponds around, garden ponds can be occupied straight away with masses of frogs looking for places to spawn. In other cases, a pond may remain unoccupied for several years, in which case it is certainly worth considering introducing frogs by putting in a few tadpoles, or half a clump of spawn from a pond where some is spare, bearing in mind that the resultant frogs will be two or three years old before they themselves spawn.

The natural lifespan of a frog is hard to determine but it is unlikely that they would survive to an enormous age. There is a record of one being kept in captivity for 12 years but 5 years is probably nearer the average. However, once a pond has become established frogs come back to it year after year. In one year they may well move a couple of miles but, more likely, it will be only 200—300 m (200—300 yards) depending on the size of the breeding colony. Where there is a large breeding colony of frogs, there is obviously a greater pressure for the inhabitants to move further afield. Much depends also on the habitat. If there is plenty of lush grass they will perhaps keep fairly close to the pond.

The reduction in the frog population has varied from area to area. In some parts of the United Kingdom it has, in the last 50 years, reduced by as much as 75 per cent to 90 per cent. In others — certainly some parts of Scotland — the percentage is not nearly so high. And there are signs that, in some suburban areas, where there are a lot of garden ponds, the population is starting to come back again. The big problem, alas, is that there are no detailed statistics on the populations of 50 years ago.

It would be a tragedy indeed if the frog were to disappear for ever, to vanish before most of us had even realised it had gone. This is one of the dangers with so many ponds being filled in. You can travel on a certain road, perhaps once a month, and grow accustomed to seeing a pond in a particular place every time you drive past, and then, suddenly, you discover that it has been filled in and that a building stands in its place. This is where local people can help. If they discover that something is going to happen — perhaps that a pond is going to be filled in — they can inform the local naturalist trust, the local museum, any interested body that is capable of taking action, if not actually to save the pond itself, possibly to save the frogs and toads which inhabit it.

In large countries such as the United States, Canada and Australia recording presents a great problem as it is difficult to organise a central pool of information. Most recording in these areas is undertaken by professionals but they could be greatly assisted by interested amateurs who understand the basic principles of objective scientific research. In addition, in those countries where collection of eggs from the wild is allowed, and where the herpetologist is confident of looking after them, rearing the young and returning populations to the wild, much can be achieved in enhancing future generations of these most maligned of creatures.

Finally, a word of warning to be careful of the species you let loose in your garden. We have been discussing in this chapter the conservation of species native to your area. The local populations of native species do not want to be suddenly over-run by some strange, foreign race of frog or toad. For example, in the Romney Marsh area of England, the Marsh Frog has taken over the habitat that the Common Frog used to inhabit. Suddenly there are very few Common Frogs and a great many Marsh Frogs. It should be noted that in many countries, including Britain, it is illegal to release non-native species into the wild and remembering always our principal concern which should be the welfare of the animals it is easy to see the reason for this widely instituted law. Both released animal, if the habitat and climate do not match its native environment, and the native animals whose prey may be threatened, are likely to suffer — a result entirely contrary to the aim of the responsible herpetologist.

9

How to obtain your pet

When, after reading this book, you have decided which pet you would like, your first move should be to contact a herpetological society or private herpetologist who will be able to advise you on the practicalities of obtaining the species of your choice.

Should, however, there not be a society in your area and the pet store is unable to assist, there are numerous avenues you can pursue, any one of which should lead to the acquisition of the reptile of your choice.

The pet department of stores such as Harrods of Knightsbridge, London, and Macy's in New York will generally undertake to supply anything from a white mouse to an elephant for customers, while zoos and veterinary surgeons can usually recommend a probable outlet.

In the United Kingdom there are a number of companies specialising in the sale of reptiles and amphibians; they import their stock worldwide and issue weekly, or irregular lists to customers. However, with impending legislation it seems likely that more and more stock will be bred in captivity and, indeed, as I write a total ban on the importation of tortoises is to come into effect from 1984.

Xenopus Ltd, Britain's largest suppliers of reptiles and amphibians, in Redhill, Surrey, produce a Buyers' Guide which they offer free to customers, while the Midland Pet Aquarium in Walsall, West Midlands, issue fortnightly lists, and run a reptilian delivery service whereby pets can be collected from the nearest railway station. Pet Mart in Mill Lane, West Hampstead, and the Regent Pet Stores in Camden Town are two useful London outlets. In Australia and New Zealand and America the societies listed (see Useful addresses, page 86) or you veterinarian will recommend local retail outlets and breeders.

How much you must be prepared to pay obviously depends on supply and demand while it goes without saying that the dealer who has had to expend a certain amount of time and money in locating and obtaining a species for you will generally expect to be rewarded somewhat more highly than the friendly hobbyist who lives round the corner.

Live foods can often be ordered from suppliers advertising in specialist magazines, enabling the keeper of reptiles and amphibians to place orders by mail if a visit to a suitable pet store is impractical.

There are obvious advantages in being able to choose the individual specimen you want as a pet. Even if you are a beginner and relatively unfamiliar with the group of animals under discussion you will be able to notice an alert and bright-eyed specimen, and you can make sure that its skin looks healthy, without wounds or parasites. If you order by mail, the company you buy from may guarantee live delivery, but they will not be responsible for the general state of health of the animal.

By far the most satisfactory way of acquiring your first pet of this group is to find local captive-bred stock. The individual animal is likely to be relatively tame, free of parasites and other diseases, and will be of a species which has proved itself tolerant of captivity. In addition, the breeder will be able to advise on suitable accommodation and food. Success with keeping a relatively easy species, and an active interest in its welfare and progress, will stand you in good stead when you want to acquire more exotic species. Remember to keep the animal's welfare your prime concern, and don't try to be too ambitious in the species you keep to begin with.

10

Herpetological societies

I have already mentioned the good sense of joining a herpetological society and a number of useful addresses are listed below (pages 86 to 88). There are, however, additional unrecorded groups springing up, and you should keep an eye open for advertisements in specialist magazines. There are also the individual hobbyists who, if approached, are usually only too happy to give the beginner the benefit of their advice.

Also, who better than the pet store trader, regularly supplying feed to clients, to ask about other reptile owners in the area, while the nearest zoo is always a good source of help and information, and your veterinary surgeon will probably pass your name on to local herpetologists if you tell him that you are keen to improve your knowledge.

To deal briefly with a number of the better known herpetological bodies one can begin by mentioning the International Herpetological Society, the objects of which are to promote an interest in reptiles and amphibians both in captivity and in the wild. Meetings are held on the first Saturday of each month in an appointed British venue, and there is a monthly newsletter mailed to members around the world which includes reports of certain items from committee meetings and news items to do with the hobby. Members' advertisements are also included (space permitting) free of charge. The I.H.S. publishes a first rate quarterly journal, *The Herptile*, and, to ease recognition between hobbyists, has available both car stickers and lapel badges, the latter being yellow in colour with a viperine snake depicted in green and gold with the letters IHS underneath.

The British Chelonia Group is another excellent society, founded about 24 years ago. Its first journal was published in 1978 and to date *Testudo* 1, 2 and 3 have been published. The objects of the group are to promote the welfare of and the interest in tortoises, terrapins and turtles both in captivity and in the wild, and to fulfil these objectives by meetings, contacts and publications. This is the only body in the United Kingdom to cater solely for the chelonia enthusiast.

The BCG provides an information service aimed at helping people who are experiencing problems with their captive specimens and, to this end, it is in close contact with a number of veterinarians with particular interests in diseases of chelonia. These vets advise on any health problems encountered by group members. Informal meetings are held at approximately two−three monthly intervals and, again, there is a newsletter, in this case, published six times a year, and containing details of meetings, short articles, correspondence, news items and veterinary notes. The journal *Testudo* comes out annually and contains articles and papers on the care, feeding, breeding, housing, maintenance, behavioural, veterinary and conservation aspects of all chelonians. A balance is deliberately aimed at between basic and more advanced articles in order to appeal to all interests while an expanding library contains books and papers, which are available to members attending meetings, or by postal loan.

The British Herpetological Society, London based, has members who are involved in a wide range of activities including the conservation and captive breeding and care of reptiles and amphibians. It produces a number of publications, including an academic journal and a semi-scientific bulletin, and has published its own book, *The Care and Breeding of Captive Reptiles.*

ASRA, the Association for the Study of Reptilia and Amphibia, is based at the Cotswold Wildlife Park in Burford, Oxford. ASRA has the following main objectives: to provide facilities for herpetologists to meet and discuss their mutual interests and to increase their knowledge of herpetological subjects by the provision of films, slides, lectures and study projects; to hold special events, such as 'open evenings' to which the general public are invited and thus nurture a more favourable attitude towards reptiles and amphibians by demonstration of their qualities; to provide members with access to a comprehensive library of books, journals, reports, papers and press clippings on all aspects of herpetology; to provide an expert herpetological information service by answering queries from the press, other media or individuals and to aid in all aspects of conservation and preservation of reptiles by educating, coordinating democratic action and raising funds to support specific projects.

In America one finds the Society for the Study of Amphibians and Reptiles, a non-profit making, international organisation, established to advance the study of amphibians and reptiles. Although begun in 1958 as a regional society, the SSAR rapidly gained a world-wide membership. Today it is recognised as having the most diverse society-sponsored programme of professional services and publications for students of herpetology. Membership is open to all persons interested in learning about amphibians and reptiles. An annual meeting is held each summer on a University campus, or at a biological station in the United States. The Society especially wishes to attract students to its meetings by providing inexpensive and informal facilities.

In addition to the papers given by members at these meetings, other speakers are usually invited and a symposium is planned which allows for detailed discussions of an important area of contemporary study. Workshops for regional society representation have been organised for the purpose of exploring common problems and sharing new ideas. Live animals and photographic art, among other exhibits, are organised as well as field trips.

The Herpetologists' League, based in Louisiana, is an international organisation of professional and amateur herpetologists dedicated to furthering knowledge of the biology of reptiles and amphibians. The league presents awards for student papers. It publishes a quarterly journal, *Herpetologica*, which is a vehicle for much of the significant herpetological research now being carried out.

Finally, there is the American Society of Ichthyologists and Herpetologists based at the Dept of Ichthyology at the American Museum of Natural History. This Society, founded in 1913, has a 2500 membership made up of scientists, educators, students and others, interested in the study of reptiles, amphibians and fish.

In addition to these national bodies, there are also a number of regional societies in America. Most states have at least one society producing regular publications and holding regular meetings locally. The larger ones, such as the Chicago Herpetological Society, the Maryland Herpetological Society and the New York Herpetological Society, all of which issue regular quarterly publications, may be of interest to herpetologists outside the immediate area.

The list of Useful addresses on pages 86 to 89 should also be consulted.

11
Legislation

Before embarking on the acquisition of an amphibian or reptile pet it is essential to determine whether a licence must be obtained for it, and the relevant authority must be satisfied as to the conditions under which the creature will be kept.

Pet store traders should all be aware of present and impending legislation. However, you will do best to check with the authorities. In Britain, the Dangerous Wild Animals Act (1976) is the responsibility of the Home Office, and in the United States the U.S. Department of the Interior, Fish and Wildlife Service will supply regulations on the keeping of animals and information on endangered species; local addresses are given in Useful addresses, (page 86). Each state, county, and city have authority to make rules or regulations on keeping certain animals either by individual owners or zoological parks. In Australia there is a total ban on the import and export of animals as pets.

There are also laws concerning the collecting and keeping of native animals, and you should make enquiries of your local herpetological society or government department once you have decided which species you would like to keep. See also Chapter 8 on recording and conserving in the wild.

Useful addresses

United Kingdom

Association of British Wild Animal Keepers, (Sec: Donald Packham), Roxburgh Cottage, Marley Place, Clifton Down, Bristol 8.

Association for the Study of Reptilia and Amphibia (ASRA), Cotswold Wild Life Park, Burford, Oxon. OX8 4JW.

Biological Records Centre, Monkswood Experimental Station, Abbots Ripton, Huntingdon.

British Chelonia Group, (Sec: Dr. R. P. Adlam), 3 Bathwick Rise, Bathwick, Bath, BA1 6RE, Avon

British Herpetological Society, c/o Zoological Society of London, Regent's Park, London NW1 4RY.

Cleveland Reptile Club, 39 Levenside, Stokesley, Cleveland.

Home Office, 50 Queen Anne's Gate, SW1.

International Herpetological Society, (Sec: A. J. Mobbs), 27 St. Thomas Close, Dartmouth Avenue, Walsall, West Midlands WS3 1SZ.

Leicester Herpetological Society, 20 Orchard Road, Birstall, Leics.

Midland Pet Aquarium Reptilium — Importers, Exporters, Wholesalers and Retailers, Specialists in Venomous Snakes, 34 Bradford Street, Walsall.

People's Dispensary for Sick Animals, PDSA House, Dorking, Surrey RH4 2LB.

Pet Mart, Mill Lane, West Hampstead, London NW6.

Regent Pet Stores, Parkway, Camden Town, London NW1.

Royal Society for the Prevention of Cruelty to Animals, (RSPCA), Causeway, Horsham, Sussex RH12 1HG.

South Western Herpetological Society, (Sec: Frank B. Gibbons), Acanthus, 59 St. Marychurch Road, Torquay, Devon.

Thames and Chilterns Herpetological Society, 21 Layters Green Lane, Chalfont St. Peter, Bucks.

Thames and Reading Herpetological Society, (Sec: Alison Barton), 41 Hatherley Road, Reading, Berkshire RG1 5QE.

Young Zoologist's Club, London Zoo, Regent's Park, London NW1 4RY.

Zoological Society of London, Regent's Park, London NW1 4RY.

United States of America

American Humane Association, 9725 East Hampden, Denver, Colorado 80231.

American Society of Ichthyologists and Herpetologists, Dept. of Ichthyology, American Museum of Natural History, New York, NY 10024.

American Society for the Prevention of Cruelty to Animals (ASPCA), 441 East 92nd Street, New York, NY 10028.

Department of Health and Human Services, Public Health Service, Centers of Disease Control, Atlanta, Georgia 30333.

Fish and Wildlife Service District Law Enforcement Offices: 1011 E. Tudor Road, Anchorage, Alaska 99501;

Lloyd 500 Building, Suite 1490, 500 N.E. Multnomah Street, Portland, Oregon 97232;

Room E 1924 2800 Cottage Way, Sacramento, California 95825;

P.O. Box 25486 DFC, Denver, Colorado 80225;

P.O. Box 1038, Independence, Missouri 64051;

P.O. Box 329, Albuquerque, New Mexico 87103;

P.O. Box 45, Twin Cities, Minnesota 55111;

546 Carondelet Street, Room 100, New Orleans, Louisiana 70130;

P.O. Box 95467, Atlanta, Georgia 30347;

P.O. Box 290, Nashville, Tennessee 37202;

95 Aquahart Road, Glen Burnie, Maryland 21061;

Century Bank Building, 2nd Floor, 700 Rockaway Turnpike, Lawrence, New York 11559;

P.O. Box 'E', Newton Corner, Massachusetts 02158.

Herpetologists' League, Dept. of Biological Sciences, Louisiana State University, In Shreveport, 8515 Youree Dr. Shreveport, LA 71115.

Society for the Study of Amphibians and Reptiles, (Sec: Dr Henri C. Selbert), Department of Zoology, Ohio University, Athens, Ohio, 45701.

Society for the Study of Amphibians and Reptiles, c/o Milwaukee Public Museum, Eighth and Wells, Milwaukee, WI 53233.

References

Books

Appleby, L. G. (1971) *British Snakes* John Baker Ltd., London.

Arnold, E. N. and Burton, J. A. (1978) *A Field Guide to the Reptiles and Amphibians of Europe* Collins, London.

Bellairs, A. (1969) *The Life of Reptiles* (2 vols) Weidenfeld and Nicolson, London.

Cochran, D. M. (1961) *Living Amphibians of the World* Doubleday Inc, New York and Hamish Hamilton, London.

Cogger, H. G. (1979) *Reptiles and Amphibians of Australia* A. H. & A. W. Reed, Sydney.

Conant, R. (1975) *A Field Guide to Reptiles and Amphibians of Eastern North America* Houghton Mifflin Co., Boston.

Gans, C. (1975) *Reptiles of the World* Ridge Press, New York.

Goin, C. J. and Goin, O. B. (1971) *Introduction to Herpetology* W. H. Freeman & Co. New York.

Kauffield, C. (1969) *Snakes: The Keeper and The Kept* Doubleday Inc, New York.

Mattison, C. (1982) *The Care of Reptiles and Amphibians in Captivity* Blandford Press, Poole, Dorset.

Phelps, T. (1981) *Poisonous Snakes* Blandford Press, Poole, Dorset.

Porter, K. R. (1972) *Herpetology* W. B. Saunders and Co., New York.

Robb, J. (1980) *New Zealand Amphibians and Reptiles* Collins, Auckland.

Schmidt, K. P. and Inger, R. F. (1957) *Living Reptiles of the World* Doubleday Inc, New York and Hamish Hamilton, London.

Stebbins, R. C. (1966) *A Field Guide to Western Reptiles and Amphibians* Houghton Mifflin Co., Boston.

Townson, S., *et al* (eds) (1980) *The Care and Breeding of Captive Reptiles* British Herpetological Society, London.

Periodicals

Bulletin of the Maryland Herpetological Society (Quarterly).

Chicago Herpetological Society Bulletin (Quarterly).

Herp (Quarterly. New York Herpetological Society).

Herpetologica (Quarterly. Herpetologists' League).

Herptile (Quarterly. International Herpetological Society).

Testudo (Annually. British Chelonia Group).

Index

Numbers in *italics* refer to
illustrations.

Abscesses 55
Abrasions 29, 67
Accommodation 7, 10, 11-13, *11-14*, 16
  alligators 34
  crocodiles 35
  frogs 25, 26-7, 30-3
  lizards 50-2, *52*, 57-8, 60-1
  newts 21-4
  salamanders 21-4
  snakes 63-6, 68, 69-70
  terrapins 43-4
  toads 25, 26-7, 30-3
  tortoises 39, 40, 41
Adder (Northern Viper) 73
Agamid lizards 48, 61
Alligator 10, 34-5
Alligator lizards 49
American Humane Association 7
American Society of Ichthyologists
  and Herpetologists 83
Amphibians 7, 8, 9-10, 25
Amphisbaenians 49
Anquid Lizards 48-9, 61
Anura 9, 10, 25, 29
Aquatic species
  newts 24

salamanders 24
toads 32
Association for the Study of Reptilia
  and Amphibia 83
Axolotl 21, *22*, 24

Basking 13, 51, *52*
Bathing
  snakes 63-4
  tortoises 39
Biological Records Centre 74-6
Blind snakes 68
Breeding 10, 25
  chameleons 49-50
  frogs 76
  mealworms for food 15
  rodents for food 15-16
  tortoises 41-2
British Chelonia Group 82
British Herpetological Society 82

Caudata 9, 10
Camouflage 48
Chameleons 47, 48, 49-50, 60
Chelonia 10
Chicago Herpetological Society 83
Classification
  amphibians 9-10, 25
  reptiles 10

91

Classification *(cont.)*
  snakes 10
Clawed Toad *28*, 32
Cleaning, 22, 43, 50, 64, 65
Cobras 10
Colds 67
Collection, indiscriminate 73
Colubrid snakes 68
Common Frog *30*, 73, 74, 77
Common Lizard 48
Common (Smooth) Newt 24, 73
Common (Viviparous) Lizard 73
Common Toad 73, 74
Conservation 72-8
Corn Snake *69*, 70
Crested Newt 24, 72
Coral snakes 10
Cottonmouth snakes 10
Crocodiles 10, 34, 35
Crocodilia 10

Dangerous Wild Animal Acts 1976 34
Data banks 74-5, 77
Dice Snake 63-4, 68
Digestion 66
Diseases 18, 29, 42, 46, 55, 67
Drinking water 15, 39, 40, 48, 63

Ears
  lizards 47
  snakes 62
Elegant Terrapin 42
Eggs
  lizard 48
  tortoise 41
European Pond Tortoise 42, 43
Eye complaints 46
Eyed Lizard 48, 61
Eyelids
  lizards 47, 62
  snakes 62

Feeding 7, 14-18, 29
  frogs 27, 30-3

lizards 47, 52-3, 57-8, 60-1
  newts 22-4
  salamanders 22-4
  snakes 15, 66-7, 68, 70-1
  tadpoles 74
  terrapins 46
toads 27, 30-3
  tortoises 39, 40-1
Financial outlay 19, 80
Fire salamanders *20*, 22, 23
Fire-bellied Newt, Japanese *21*, 24
Fire-bellied Toad
  Giant *29*
  Oriental *28*, 33
Food reserves 55
Four-lined snake *69*, 70
Frogs 7, 9-10, 25-33
  characteristics 9-10, 25
  origins 25
  population studies 77
  species suited to captivity 30-3
  varieties 25
Furnishings for vivaria 23-4, 26-7,
    30-3, 57-8, 60-1, 63-4, 68
  island 26, 43
  pond 27, 43
  shelter 13, 51, 63
  substrate 13, 27, 64
  vegetation 13, 27, 43, 51

Gangrene 42, 55
Garter Snake *63*, 64, 68
Gecko 47, 49, 53, 57
  Kotschy's *49*
  Kuhl's *50*, 57
  Leopard *55*, 57
Giant Toad 26
Glass lizards 49
Grass Snake 64, 73
Green Anole *56*, 58
Green Lizard 48, 61
Gulf Coast Toad *27*

Habitat destruction 73

Handling 22, 34
Heating 11, 12, 29, 64
Hermann's Tortoise 37, 38, 40
Herpetologists' League 83
Hibernation 39-40
Horned lizard 50, 51-2
Humidity 11, 12, 21, 50, 51
Hygiene 22

Iguana 48, 55, 58
  Curly-tailed 53
  Green 54
International conventions 72
International Herpetological Society
    81
Introduced species 77-8
Invertebrate food 16, 17

Komodo Dragon 49
Lacertid lizards 48, 60-1
Legislation 11, 34, 78, 85
Life-cycle 10, 39-40
Lifespan
  chameleons 49-50
  frogs 76
  lizards 47
Lighting 12, 21, 29, 35, 49, 64
Lizards 10, 20, 47-61
  characteristics 47
  origins 47
  species suited to captivity 57-8, 60-1
  varieties 48-9, 50

Mambas 10
Marsh Frog 77, 78
Maryland Herpetological Society 83
Mealworms 27, 52
  breeding for food 16, 17
Mediterranean Spur-thighed
    Tortoise 38
Minerals 18, 35, 42, 52, 53
Mole salamanders 21
Monitor lizards 48
Mouth rot 55, 67

Natterjack Toad 72, 73
Natural environment 9, 20, 43, 51, 74
New York Herpetological Society 83
Newts 9, 20-4, 25
  characteristics 20
  origins 21
  species suited to captivity 23-4

Origins
  frogs 25
  lizards 47
  newts 21
  salamanders 21
  toads 25
  tortoises 38

Palmate Newt 23, 24, 73
Parasites 7, 37, 42, 46, 67
Pesticides 76
Pit vipers 10
Plated lizards 48, 61
Poison arrow frogs 25, 31
Pollution 73
Ponds, artificial 75-6
Pneumonia 67
Protected species 34, 72, 73
Publications 7, 10, 39, 67, 79, 80, 81,
    82

Racerunner lizards 48, 50
Rattlesnakes 10
Records 18
Recording 72-8
Red Eft 21, 23
Redleg 29
Reed Frog, Marbled 27, 31
Reptiles 7, 8, 9, 10-11
Ribbon Snake, Western 64
Rodents, breeding for food 15-16

Salamanders 9, 20-4, 25
  characteristics 20
  origins 21
  species suited to captivity 23-4

Salmonellosis 22
Sand Lizard 48, 72, 73
Security 21, 65
Semi-aquatic species
  frogs 33
  newts 24
  toads 33
Sexing
  lizards 48, *48*
  tortoises 38, *38*
  terrapins 43
Shell, terrapin 42, 43
Shell, tortoise 38
  injury 42
Size
  alligators 34
  lizards 46, 52
  snakes 62
  tortoises 38
Skin complaints 15, 29, 67
Skinks 48, 58
  Five-lined *51*, 58
Slough failure 67
Slow Worm 48, 61, 73
Smooth Snake 72, 73
Snakes 7, 10, 15, 62-71
  history 62
  characteristics 62-3
  species suited to captivity 68
Snout abrasion 55
Societies 7, 79, 80, 81-4
Society for the Study of Amphibians
    and Reptiles 83
Spanish Terrapin 42, 43
Spawn 7
Species suited to captivity
  frogs 30-3
  lizards 57-8, 60-1
  newts 23-4
  salamanders 23-4
  snakes 68
  toads 32-3

Squamata 10
Suppliers 7, 22, 38, 50, 79-80, 81, 86

Temperature requirements 9, 12, 34,
    35, 41, 46, 49, 50, 51, 57, 64, 65
Tegus 48
Terrapins 10, 36, 42-6
  characteristics 42
  species suited to captivity 42
Terrestrial species
  frogs 30-2
  newts 23
  salamanders 23
  toads 30-2
Toads 7, 9-10, 25-33
  characteristics 25
  origins 25
  species suited to captivity 30-4
Tortoises 10, 36-42
  importation 79
  origins 36, 38
Tree-dwellers, furnishings for 13, 51
Tree Frogs 25, 26, 31, 32
  Grey *26*, 31
  Pacific *26*, 31
Turtles 10

Veterinary care 18, 19, 29, 42, 55, 67
Vine Snake 15
Vipers 10
Vitamins 18, 35, 41, 42, 52, 55

Wall Lizard 48, *56*, 60
Warty (Great Crested) Newt 24, 73
Water Snake, Green *65*, 70
Whiptails 48, 50
Wildlife and Countryside Act of
    1981 72
Woodland salamanders 21

Zonures 48, 60